NO REGRETS

THE JOURNEY

Hector LaFosse

Stay True

H. LaFosse

Visit our website at www.StillwaterPress.com for more information.

First Stillwater River Publications Edition

ISBN-13: 978-1-946-30070-6
ISBN-10: 1-946300-70-5

Library of Congress Control Number: 2018950430

1 2 3 4 5 6 7 8 9 10

Written by Hector LaFosse
Cover design by Nathanael Vinbury
Published by Stillwater River Publications, Pawtucket, RI, USA.

I have tried to recreate events, locales and conversations from my memories of them. In order to maintain their anonymity in some instances I have changed the names of individuals and places, I may have changed some identifying characteristics and details such as physical properties, occupations and places of residence.

This is the tale of an adult who carried the hurt child and the angry teen within, through a tumultuous life of jail, drug wars, and the struggle for survival against all odds to overcome and find peace and success within.

DEDICATION

This book is dedicated to my sons.

S pecial thanks to Debra Koffler my friend and producer, who helped me with my manuscript. Thank you. It is your unwavering support that lit the flame under my feet. Henry Medina, my longtime friend and brother that never let me quit and always had my back. To Jaime Osorno for all your help. To Piri Thomas for planting the SEED with, "Down These Mean Streets. To Magda; Counselor and Director at Narco Freedom, that always told me, I didn't belong there, and I could do better. To **Rafael Rivera-Viruet**; my Mentor-thank you. To my friend Eugene Pinto for the trust and bond we built and your support in this journey. I will miss you. And, most of all, to my wife Sylvia for believing in me and seeing me through the rough times, and the long nights when she had to bring me to bed after writing all night.

In loving memory of my parents Ramon & Francisca Laffosse,
and to my cousin Luis M. Fosse RIP

Table of Contents

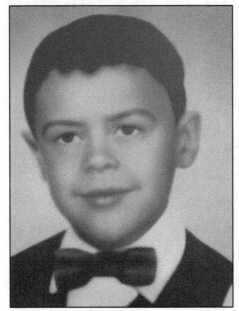

A kid with a dream.

Mom and Pop.

INTRODUCTION

I have little use for my past except to use its lessons to propel me forward. However, it is because of the past that this book came into existence. Until the age of thirty-nine I pretty much lived a non-existent life. I lived in a state of anxiety and depression with suicidal thoughts constantly plaguing me. It feels now as if I'm talking about someone else, because it's so difficult to see that it was me. It seems a lifetime away. At times it's difficult to accept why I stayed there all that time when it was just hurting me.

One night while staring at the ceiling, it all came back to me in a flash, and I was looking at my whole life as images, like in a movie reel. I tried switching the channel in my head, but the scenes kept playing, like I was living them out over and over again. It was a feeling of absolute dread, and pain that was more intense than the actual experience itself. I felt a void within, and a deep loathing for myself. I would blink, and turn to stare elsewhere to try and interrupt my thoughts, only to pick them up again, and feel more of the dread. Despair arose, and I became hostile. In a moment of anger I got up and began breaking things; throwing around anything my hands could reach. My life felt utterly meaningless and the self-loathing took over. I had no self-worth. There was no point continuing living with the miserable burden of life God gave me. Why carry on this way? Everything was a continuous struggle. I felt totally isolated from the world around me, as my anger went to a deeper level. I could not live with myself any longer. I was locked onto a fixed idea, and in my mind I played out the scene. Then suddenly, I became aware I was thinking about taking my life, and that thought frightened me. I was gripped with an intense fear and my body began shaking. I felt drained, so I closed my eyes to try to relax myself, and I ended up falling asleep. When I awoke, I thought it was all a dream. I sat up, looked at the cell bars, and I began to cry.

I was stunned as I realized how many years I spent carrying these issues around, where it got me and where it almost took me. It wasn't just about the jail cell, but the prison I had built within—those walls were even harder to tear down, because my skin grew tougher as I kept having similar experiences. It was the stuff within which was killing me. Until I dealt with those feelings, my life was going to become a revolving door to pain.

As humans, we are conditioned to hang on and tough things out. We are supposed to put an "H" on our chest and "handle it." Some of us suffer in secrecy, ashamed to tell our secrets, out of fear we may be judged, or be made vulnerable. This sends our very existence out of whack. It would take a lot for me to begin looking at myself; besides, I really didn't know where to begin. It was easier to just not go there and continue feeling the way I was, hoping it would pass, or that I would just wake up one day and never think about it again.

As the years continued to pass, the feelings and thoughts remained. At that point, I knew I wouldn't be able to continue living my life this way. Even after acknowledging this, the thought of moving into an area of uncharted territory was frightening. At first, I was filled with fear and dread, then suddenly something profoundly significant happened. The instant I surrendered from fighting, I began to feel lighter and more positive. I began to experience hope. It was as if the light switch came on and I was being released from the demons that robbed me of life. So, the work began. It was in that moment that my life turned around.

Although deeply unhappy and reluctant to disclose at times, I remained steadfast. I was finally exposing my secrets, and as I became more transparent, the intense pressure of suffering and fear of self-discovery was getting easier. My outlook about the world began to change. I was no longer blaming society, my upbringing, my parents, or all of those that caused me harm as a child. It was really rough at first. Letting go was a task. Forgiving myself and others was difficult. Being nice and loving myself was a foreign feeling. The change was happening. Laughter and glimpses of happiness were showing up. I was being transformed before my own eyes.

A time came when, for a while, I had nothing. My relationship was not working, I had no job, nothing on the physical plane, barely a place to live, and no socially defined identity. I spent most times alone, yet these were some of my best moments. In my solitude, I have found some relief and a little peace. I am no longer beating on myself for the wasted time or errors of my past.

This book represents me and the freedom that I've experienced since the disclosure of my truth. I wrote it because of the deep dissatisfaction within me, and I knew no other way to free myself but through sharing my story. For a long time, I thought about writing about my life—and three years ago it exploded inside me. While it makes for a good read, and entertainment, there is also a message. I hope you get as much out of it, as I intended.

There are many people out there experiencing the same lifestyle and still suffering with some form of addiction. Maybe some get addicted to numb themselves so they don't have to feel anything. Some people with low self-esteem and abandonment issues get caught up in relationships seeking love just to feel wanted. Rape victims usually end up having children at a very young age, complicating their lives even more. Others stay in abusive relationships that validate their past experiences. Many young boys that experience sexual assault grow up angry and become very bitter, while others have taken their own lives without ever having the opportunity to free themselves from these deep secrets.

For those that can identify and are ready to commit the same mistakes—this book is for you. You can change, end the suffering so you can move on with life. The struggle is real and although rehabilitation can seem like forever, you are well worth the effort. Although you may not be fully ready to release your pain, maybe when the pain becomes greater, you will remember me, and you will choose life instead of misery.

I want to share my authentic story. I want to use this as a platform for hope, and give voice to all those that have died with their secrets. I want to bring acceptance, and love, to say, "you can if you want to,"—nothing is impossible, no matter how grim things may seem. Dream and fight on. Don't make excuses for where you're at in your life. Change your thinking to change your life. Don't isolate yourself. You are not damaged goods. The possibilities are endless if you believe in them.

Some of what you read here may surprise you. It may also be sensitive and strike a chord with you. My intention is not to offend, hurt, or bring up pain.

I apologize in advance if I shock, or hurt you in any way, for this is not my intention.

This is my book, my story, my life....

So much more unsaid, as I lived through this hell,
but for now, I leave you with this….

CHAPTER 1

Lil-Man

The Brooklyn Bridge.

My name is Pepe Santos. Born in East New York, I am the second youngest of seven siblings. For a while, we had great times growing up in Brooklyn. If you were a kid, Georgia Avenue was where you wanted to be. There were three story homes along with five story tenement buildings. We spent hours on the stoops, in the hallway flipping and matching baseball cards, or playing tops. As kids we were daring. We would slow down or stop traffic, while we made boxes with chalk in the middle of the street. It was a series of squares from one to twelve and a box in the center with a thirteen called "The Scully." That was the penalty area you didn't want to fall into, unless you went through every box first to become king. Sometimes we played Scully till we missed supper. There were games like "Johnny-on-the-Pony," "Kick-The-Can," "Ringo-a-livio," "Stickball" and many others. The girls had their own games, like jumping rope—called "Double Dutch," or played Hopscotch. Sometimes, they'd just watch us play. Other times, we'd go to the abandoned buildings to jump out a second story window onto mattresses below. As we got a little bigger, the games became more dangerous. We'd go from jumping lumber in Ridgewood to jumping rooftops. To escape from the world, we would hang out on the rooftop. There was something cool about being on top of the world with nothing but sky above us. Up there, we would dream, tell stories and fantasize about what we wanted to be when we grew up. Sometimes we'd fill a bag of balloons with water at the fire hydrant, take them up to the roof and blast people below. Most of us never left the block, so the rooftop became our beach to hang out and get a sun tan, or just watch all the movement below. Many of the guys began building pigeon coops and that became a pastime. Summer time was the best time. The energy was everywhere, and it was like being a flower in full bloom. The streets were our playground from sunrise to sundown. There was no lack of imagination, and no stipulations to our days except to be a kid and have fun.

Once, I saw a picture of one of my uncles in Puerto Rico. He was on a horse in full police uniform. I only met him once before he died of cancer, but my childhood dream was to become a cop like him. He was nothing like my disabled father who lost his dry-cleaning business in a fire, and took to drinking every day. Pops would stay home, talk to himself, and blare that old Spanish music. He ruled with an iron fist.

My mother was a loving, religious woman. She was soft, kind and most times very quiet. She always appeared to be listening and analyzing things. Her form of communication was with her eyes. We all knew when she disagreed with something we were doing. Although she didn't talk much, she always told me I had a big heart and to follow it. She always told me the truth and spoke about God.

She was very protective about her cubs. Two to three nights a week a van would come pick us all up and we'd go to the Pentecostal church. I always kicked and screamed because I hated going, and listening to all those Spanish Christian songs, or yelling "Hallelujah." made me ill. I sat there with a mop on my face and my arms across my chest like I was dying. I'd rather have been home playing with some toys or watching cartoons. Sometimes, I would get with the other children who felt the same way and we would run around interrupting the service. I was always being pulled by the ear back into my seat. My other siblings would just look at me as if I was a retard. I didn't know how to stay still—poor Mom. She had all the patience in the world, but I could see how I frustrated and embarrassed her. I recall at the beginning how Mom would convince Pop to go, hoping God would help him and he would stop drinking. Pop was a slick dresser. He would get dressed with his suit and tie and although he often smiled, he appeared just as bored. He only did it to please Mom, but he was always a pain in the ass. I could not move when he came, and with the two-hour service, it was easier to just die.

Pops picked up a routine of waking my mom up in the middle of the night to cook for him. We all kind of already knew where this was going and it made us nervous. He would get mad and start arguing with Mom. Dishes were thrown against the wall regularly. He would pick fights with her and become physically abusive. In the beginning, we would all wake up, but everyone got used to it after a while. I didn't know how my brothers could shut it out, but I never could. The noise was too loud in my head. I would end up getting out of bed to intervene. Whenever he beat Mom in front of me, I held onto his leg, and he would drag me around trying to get me off, until finally he'd beat on me too. This went on three or four times a week for years. I recall a feeling of bitterness, sadness and anger, balling up my fist wanting to punch a wall. We begged Mom to leave but she wouldn't. She was old school and believed in the whole "till death do us part" thing. Many days I felt sorry for her. Whenever he drank, she lived in fear for her safety and ours. To protect her from his rages, I'd step in, and take all the beatings I could stand.

Going to school every day was difficult. I was always tired from the night before. I couldn't focus on the little work assignments, and while the kids played games, I wanted to sleep. My teacher would always ask me, "Is there something wrong at home?"

I would lie saying, "No, teacher, I was up watching TV late."

Over summer break in the mid '60s despite my objections, my Mom would send me off to my uncle's place in upper Manhattan on 177th Street to get me away from everything I was witnessing. Here, in uptown Manhattan, all the buildings were five and six story tenements. My uncle was cool. Together he and I built my very first bike from used parts. That was when I met my best friend Renzo, who lived around the corner also in a basement apartment. Our buildings were back to back, with an alley separating them. Most times we'd see one another in the back alley, which we called the "yard." Often times it's where we played. After standing around watching me and my uncle, I invited him over to help us with the bike, and since he didn't have one, it became "our" bike. That summer, we both got a little hustle at the E&B supermarket on Broadway packing bags for tips. This was when we shared our first cigarette. The bus terminal was directly across the street and became our playground. We would ride on the escalators and run around all day. We had a lot of fun. When summer ended, I was sent back home. Somehow, I always knew I would see him again, but I sure was going to miss him.

We were a very poor family living on welfare. I remember always wanting a birthday party like the average kids, but I can't say I ever had one. In fact, the only picture I have as a child was a school picture after graduating from kindergarten, and that was torn up by my baby sister, Cindy, as a child. We survived eating the cheese and peanut butter they gave out at the community center. Since Pop lost the dry cleaners, he didn't work anymore.

He would take the last of our welfare dollars and go to the liquor store up the block. A bottle of Imperial was his liquor of choice to get drunk. The employees knew him so well at the liquor store that when he couldn't get out of bed, he would call and then send me to pick up a bottle for him. I would spike it with water sometimes because I was afraid of what was coming if he got too drunk. Some days he was able to tell and would ask if I had done something to it. Of course, I would deny it.

Pop knew everybody in the neighborhood. The coolest cats to know where the grocery store owners; they gave Pop credit when we had no money, and when Mom got her welfare check, Pop would buy his liquor, get buzzed up, and then go pay Don Pacheco at the grocery store. Sundays after supper was a special day for us as a family. We would all sit at the kitchen table to wait for Pop to show up with a coconut cake and a container of milk; Mom loved coconut cake. Every Sunday without fail, Pop would come through. Many times our bill would get too high at the store, and I would hear Don Pacheco arguing with Pop about the note. The store was our lifeline, and Mom did everything she could to save grace, but Pop, well, he needed his bottle.

I used to be embarrassed going to school with my brother's hand-me-downs. The sneakers had to be stuffed with newspaper to fit me, and cardboard lined the bottom to cover the holes. My mother tried hard to comfort me because I was always angry. I cried a lot because of the shame, and the kids at school teasing me did not help. I hated school because of the humiliation I felt, and I started fighting at a very young age. My teachers knew the situation; they liked me and tried to shelter me from all of the mean comments.

My second-grade teacher came to visit me at home once because I was sick with the mumps. She brought a guitar and sang to me. I was instantly in love for the first time. I remember crying when I graduated to third grade because she wouldn't be my teacher any longer. I wanted to stay in the second grade forever. My heart was broken.

The most peaceful loving moments I could remember were when my mother would pick me up from school. She would hold my hand, smile at me and then we would take the long way home. I always knew what that smile meant. Sometimes we'd just sit in the park to listen to the birds chirp.

Those happy feelings were always short-lived because we both knew what awaited us once we got home.

At times my dad would be outside after drinking his ass off, and the guys on the block would challenge him to do dumb things. He would entertain them by blowing up firecrackers with his fingers, and then drink some more to numb the pain. Other times, they'd be outside our window placing bets and waiting for him to start throwing things out in his drunken tirade. Pops could usually be found sitting on a board with a milk crate on each end until mom got her welfare check and repurchased furniture. Everyone in the neighborhood knew us. The elders felt sorry for us while the youngsters laughed. For recreation, the dads would go up the block to the super's basement at 557 and put boxing gloves on us to fight. Afterwards, the fighting continued in the streets during games whenever there was a disagreement, or when the teenagers encouraged us—everyone always wanted to see a fight.

About the age of six I was sexually molested at my friend's house by his older brother. I remember fighting and crying for him to let me go. My friend did nothing to help me. I thought maybe he was experiencing the same abuse because he seemed scared too, but I was still so mad at him. I was only a block away from home, but I can remember it was the longest walk ever. At no time did I look up, my head was faced down towards the ground. I walked the whole way home mad and in tears, feeling like my world had just been shattered into a million pieces. I felt helpless and humiliated, regretting that I had allowed myself to be put in that situation, blaming myself the entire time. I've lived with the pain of that memory ever since. I was afraid to tell anyone because I didn't know how. Mostly, I didn't think anyone would believe me. I became very confused by the emotions I was experiencing so I locked myself in my own little world. Every time the memory of that moment surfaced, I would push it down and angrily deny it ever happened. It was an ongoing battle within myself as I kept reliving the moment. I did everything I could think of to help me forget, but nothing I tried worked. I was haunted by that experience, and it affected my whole life. My spirit became dark and full of hate. The experience literally destroyed my psyche, sending my life into a tailspin that set the tone for what was to come in my life. I remember saying to myself "when I get older I'm going to find him and kill him."

Something within me had changed. My self-esteem plummeted and I felt broken and ashamed. That was when I first remember wearing the mask to help me hide my weakened self. It protected me from the external world of cruelty and punishment. I couldn't trust anyone, and would let no one in. At first I wore the mask to shelter my emotions, but then it would also come in handy to isolate myself from my true self. I crawled back into a world I created where I felt safe and no one could hurt me. Thereafter, the mask became the norm. Deep down inside, there was still this looming fear that I hid from the world with the mask as it grew tighter, chiseled on my face. It was difficult enough coming from New York City where everyone had to show some kind of toughness, but as I died spiritually, not really caring about anything became easier. The experiences were painful, and I continued blocking the painful memories by wearing the mask full time, while I kept my secrets buried.

I convinced my mom to let me stay out a little later to work so that I could help her out. Pop thought it was a good idea, so he helped me build a shoe shine box, took me to buy the things I needed, and then taught me how to give a good shine—I was so excited. I stationed myself on Livonia Avenue under the L train and took my first job. I shined a few shoes and made some money, then headed home where my father counted my money and helped himself to most of it. I learned his ways and the next time, before I went home, I made sure to go to the Jewish store across the street to buy some dill pickles directly from the barrel and stuff my face. Man, I loved those pickles. After a while, I wouldn't even tell him how much I made and I would take all that extra money and add it to my piggy bank. This was probably the first time I had knowingly manipulated my dad.

It was during that same summer at the age of seven that I had my first sexual encounter with a female. She was a seventeen-year-old that lived along the same sidewalk as me at 557 Georgia Avenue. She called me from her third floor window to ask me to help her clean her house while her parents were out. I gladly went up, and instead of cleaning, she approached me slowly and pulled down my pants, as I stood there a little nervous with an erection. She threw me on the couch and took advantage of me. I remember feeling in love for the second time. Every day I stood by her window waiting for her to call me again. When she called, it was for one of the bigger guys to help her. Again, I was disappointed and heartbroken.

It wasn't long before we moved to the Bushwick section of Brooklyn on Madison Avenue. It appeared somewhat different from East New York where most of the buildings were five stories. Here there were smaller buildings, only two to three stories high, and the whole landscape was different. There were many trees lining each side of the street giving it this serene and pretty feeling. Even the air had a certain fresh spring smell to it.

Although a part of me was sad moving out and missing my friends, I was also looking forward to a happy, new start on life. Mom enrolled me in the Public School at P.S.106 on Wilson Avenue. As early as the fourth grade, I remember cutting class, going to a friend's house while their parents were out or at work, and making out with our girlfriends with our coats over our heads. I still remember my girl's name, Mimi. She was my girl, that is, until her big brother and father found out that she was cutting class, and I never saw her again. I looked for her in school, I went around her block and asked for her and no one knew. Just like that she vanished, and my heart was broken for a third time. School was never the same without her and I was the only one from the crew without a girl.

When we didn't cut class to be with the girls, we would sneak onto the train and go explore different sections of Brooklyn. Crossing into Bensonhurst, we were chased by a group of bigger kids calling us spics and niggers. As we walked faster, they began chasing us; my heart was racing and we began booking it out of there. I ran as fast as I could, but two of our guys got caught and were beat up. I felt horrible leaving them, but everyone was on their own, and there were too many of them. We watched helplessly from a distance until they got tired of punching and kicking them and they left them laying on the ground bleeding. We nervously went back to help them out of there and headed home. I was so angry, and perplexed; I said, "Why would they do this?"

When Curtis, one of the two black guys said, "Because they are white and we are not." It didn't make any sense to me because I never knew the difference.

The following day at school, I couldn't help myself but look around and realize that there were no white people there. Back in the neighborhood,

I decided to take notice of white people and realized I could actually count them on one hand, even though they lived every day as a part of us. We had the same experience while going into Ridgewood when a group of white guys began yelling "You niggers, get the fuck out of our area." We continued walking and they began chasing us, only this time, we didn't run far before we turned around and started fighting. We couldn't stay out of Ridgewood being that Bushwick was connected and so close to home, but every time we went, it was with more guys. Bensonhurst was another story—we stayed out of there altogether. I couldn't get why people hated others that didn't look like them. I knew I was Spanish but to me it didn't make a difference. Racism and segregation became very real and a part of everyday life even into adulthood.

Things were feeling better, but just when I thought everything was going to be alright, Pop started his shit all over again. I was losing my fucking mind. I wanted to run away, but I couldn't leave Mom alone; I was her protector. My oldest brother, Jimbo, moved out to live with his real father who came looking for him after many years. It was the first time he ever met him. His dad had a store on Miller Avenue and my brother started working there. Mom was happy for him, but Pop, he was hurt, pissed and jealous. My brother always knew my dad as his father, and Pop treated him the best. Of course, I never knew that Pop was not his real dad, nor did anyone else for that matter. Every month, my brother would bring us groceries and gifts. It felt strange not having him at home, and although I was glad to see him, it felt strange when he would visit. His father was a very nice man who welcomed my other older brother Ed as his own and gave him a job at his store as well.

I once had the courage to ask my mother why she left my brother's dad to marry Pop. Her reply was, "Then I wouldn't have had you." Mom never shared any of her feelings. Even when Pop would beat her, she would always say, "I'm alright." She tried sheltering us from her pain. Even though she never really communicated with us or said, "I love you," to any of us, we all knew she did. She was always concerned for us and looked me in the eye as if she was reading me. She worried most for me—maybe she knew I would become the lost one.

We grew up knowing everything, without ever sharing anything. Everything was a secret, and we were not allowed to talk about what went on at home. Still, I suffered from a lack of love and affection. I'm sure my siblings felt the same. I didn't understand the emotion, but I knew I was longing for it. I sought love in all the wrong places, with the wrong people, for the wrong reasons—man, was I confused. I thought mothers were supposed to provide love and affection, and fathers would provide guidance on how to become a man. Maybe I was expecting too much from my parents.

A day came that Pop physically hurt Mom very badly. I called my big brother Jimbo and told him. When my brother rushed over, he saw Pop passed out drunk on the sofa. He picked up a lead pipe and beat him with it. My brother broke his skull, arm and ribs. He threw him out of the house and down a flight of stairs. I stood there and watched in bewilderment as I saw my dad lying helplessly in a pool of blood. I really didn't want my brother to hurt him. I almost felt sorry for Pop and my first instinct was to run down and help him to his feet, but my brother grabbed my little arm to hold me back. My brother told him, "I will kill you the next time you put a hand on our mother." The cops came and Pop told them he tripped and fell. I saw the tears in my mom's eyes and began feeling sorry for her as well. It hurt me to see Pop go into the ambulance all alone. It was the first time I ever witnessed such violence. Pop chilled for a long time after that. Although he continued drinking, the hitting stopped. He became a little withdrawn. Whenever my brother would visit, Pop knew ahead of time and would leave the house until my brother was gone. I felt a little sad for him, but, from then on, I was more comfortable leaving Mom and my baby sister Cindy alone with him.

It wasn't long before I made new friends. We started hanging out on Myrtle Avenue and Wyckoff where the "L" train ran overhead. It was a busy area with a lot of stores and bars. It was predominantly Irish. Every day we waited for the newspaper to hit the stand, paid a nickel for each one and headed to the Irish pubs to sell them for a quarter. All night long, we ran back and forth until the papers at the newsstand ran out. Most of the men at the bar were drunk. They saw us as nice little kids, and would even tip us. Little did they know, we weren't so nice. We took advantage when they were drunk. While one of us distracted them, the other would slip their money off the counter and hurry out. We would then go to the Italian pizzeria, have a slice with extra cheese, or a Sicilian, a root beer soda and stuff our faces. There was nothing like a N.Y. slice. We had pizza places all over. It was the cheapest and most filling meal that we could never get enough of. We had so much fun making money. Mom was always concerned, but I assured her I was alright, and she tolerated it, probably to keep me away from Pop.

I was making so much money, I began buying my own clothes and helping Mom out behind Pop's back. Pop didn't care where the money was coming from as long as the first thing I did when I came through the door was pass some of it to him. Nothing else mattered to him. I knew how to get around him now, so I would come home late, if I came home at all. By then, I was doing what I wanted and when I wanted. No one was able to control me and I thought I was a man. I even called myself, "Lil-Man," (Little man). It became my first tag name.

CHAPTER 2

Glue Sniffing & Shoplifting

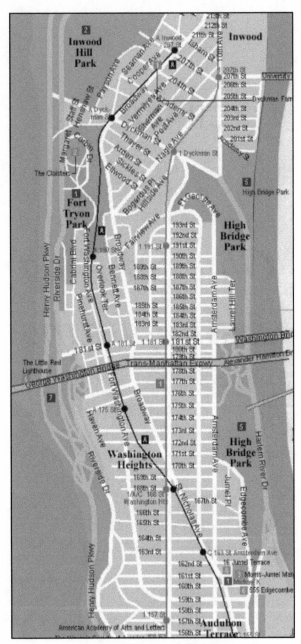

A map of Washington Heights.

Every minute out of the house was an escape. I was nine years old and already felt like I was becoming independent. Pop and I were having issues. The abandoned homes on Madison and Wilson Avenues became my hang out. We had the same crew from school that hung out regularly: Ray, Teddy, Teddy's sister Sally, Pauli, little Clyde, Curtis and me. It first started with the "Prince glue," when putting together car or airplane models alone in my room. It had this distinct smell I was attracted to, and I found myself wanting to work on the models just to open the tube of glue that came with it. Whenever I had some extra money, I went to buy a new model. I was doing this so much that my parents found it peculiar I was spending a lot of time at home locked in my room. Then, after sharing with the guys, I learned that most of them were doing the same, so we thought it was a good idea to just go out and purchase the glue without the model. We poured the glue in a small one-pound double paper bag, cuffed the top over and began sniffing in silence until our ears buzzed and then we sank into oblivion. Sometimes we'd stay there for hours. We were doing this just about every day. It was also the time we all took to shoplifting, which helped us to continue supporting our new habit.

Pop and my brother Jimbo had reconciled, so Pop would often call him to let him know what was going on with me. If my brothers weren't dragging me home, it was the cops that brought me. Every time I got home, I faced a brutal punishment. One time, Pop cleared the room of all the furniture, locked the door, and stripped me of my clothes. He had me kneel down on rice grains, with my hands up, and placed a book on each hand. Whenever I lowered my arms, he would strike me with a TV cord across my bottom. Mom would scream her lungs out on the other side of the door begging him to stop as she heard my cries. I realized then how much I hated my dad, and I knew it wouldn't be long before I left home for good.

15

I was always a tough kid. I wanted to be independent. One summer day while everyone was asleep, I decided to run away. I took off to the abandoned buildings where I used to sniff glue. There were other kids already staying there, in half a block of empty three-story row homes that were joined together. We were all happy to see one another and it gave us comfort being together. Some of us had used mattresses where we slept huddled up together, while others slept on the floor or on chairs. We made holes through the walls to go from house to house without leaving the building. We tied fishing wire to staircases with spoons to alert us when someone was coming so we had time to flee. The only time we would go outside was at night to search for food, or to take a bath every few days at a fire hydrant or at a friend's house when their parents were out. We would wait for the bread truck to make the delivery at Bohack Supermarket at three am in the morning. The driver would open the gates to the supermarket and slide in trays full of fresh baked bread and cakes. Once he left, we would pull the trays with a clothes hanger until we could reach the goods. We squeezed what we could through the little diamond opening on the gate and stuffed our bags. Not once did I ever come out with a whole cake, but the fresh, hot smelling Italian bread came out easy and lasted us a few days. We picked up stolen milk bottles delivered to the doorstep of private homes, and with our bare hands we tore into the cake and bread like hungry wolves. Other times we would put rubber bands at the bottom of our pants, walk into the supermarket and stuff our pants with food while the others blocked anyone's view, then walk out the same way.

I stayed gone for months. My mother and sisters were looking for me. I heard my mother and sisters calling my name going from building to building. I'd hide behind the wall and peep out the corner of a broken window so I could see them. I could see the pain in Mom's eyes and the hurt in her voice as she stood there. My heart was tearing apart as I cried silently with her. I prayed she would hurry up and leave because the pain of watching her was too intense. When she'd finally go, I would drop to the ground and bawl my eyes out. Some of my friends saw how much she cared and how much she was suffering, and told me I should go back home, but I wasn't ready to go back, I was having a lot of fun. I was also not looking forward to seeing my dad and dealing with the ass whipping that awaited me.

Every day Mom did the same thing—she knew I was there, and it was becoming harder and harder to handle. While I was out once, I ran into my little sister Cindy. I showed her where to find me, but I told her not to tell anyone. She began bringing me snacks or some coins she'd take from my dad's pocket when he got drunk. She kept her promise and never told a soul. I loved her so much. I always had the feeling that one day I would be taking care of her. One day Mom showed up in tears again, calling out for me, only this time she stayed longer—which even had my friends crying and saying they wished their parents cared as much. I couldn't stand hurting her anymore, and I finally went out to meet her. I was dirty and scared as I walked toward her. She ran and grabbed me into her arms, and we both cried. She took me by the hand as she always did, and led me home in silence.

When I returned home, my mother and siblings begged Pop to leave me alone. Mom made me a hot bath, fed me, and then put me to bed. Nothing was the same after that. Everything was quiet. It felt strange being back home; almost as if I no longer belonged there. I remember feeling empty; it was as if something inside me had broken. I had changed.

I didn't care what anyone had to say, and often I disobeyed Pop's rules. When he grounded me, I would sneak out my window and stay gone the entire night. In the morning, I'd wait until someone exited the building and then creep back in. I pretended I left early to throw out the garbage, but Pop would always find out and things just got worse. The beatings had little effect on me, they would just make me angry. Once I even told him to hit me harder when already he had me kneeling in a corner of the room. That really pissed him off and he went into a rage, whipping me as I stood there in pain, crying and feeling hate with every lash. One time I disturbed him during a domino game he was losing, so he picked me up and slammed me to the ground. His friends were all in shock as they came to my assistance. Mom finally had enough and sent me away again, this time to live with my older brother Jimbo, his new wife Mary and their two kids in the Bedford Stuyvesant part of Brooklyn.

Mary lived directly above us as kids. I knew her long before she became my brother's wife. She had taken in her sister Nelly because their stepfather had been abusing her for years. Nelly and I became close. When not in the living room, I slept in the same room as her on a little folding cot. We were like siblings. Her boyfriend Ray and his brother Larry lived across the hall. They became my best friends.

Ray, Larry, and I were always hanging out in the hallway. Their mother treated me well, and I slept in their house on many nights. She knew from the kids that Mary never cooked and, that I was uncomfortable living there. Mary was on a diet, therefore, so was everyone else. Ray and Larry's mom was a great cook, and she would feed me well. When given permission, we began hanging outside. I thought I was the shit so I didn't like the feeling of having to ask for permission. Although I was

The George Washington Bridge.

a young boy, asking for permission made me feel like a little kid when my thinking was that of an older person—so I thought. I hated following rules, but I did so because of my brother, and I was the newest member of his household. I was unhappy.

My brother worked late hours to take care of everyone. When he would come home he'd come directly to me and ask me how I was doing. I would never tell him the truth. He knew very little of what was happening in the house. Mary was having an affair. It felt shitty not telling him, but she warned me not to. The brothers next door were my only solace. We joined Mary's new boyfriend's karate crew. It was called "The Taekwondo Brothers." We practiced Tae-kwon-do as if we were in a karate school, but we were a clique of punk thugs. While in Highland Park one day practicing Taekwondo, a group of white guys ran into us and a big fight broke out. We had nunchucks, so we beat the crap out of them. We took off when one of them got hurt really bad, and with a bigger crew they came looking for us. Mary got scared and told my brother, and once again, I was shipped off to my uncle's house to finish out the summer.

My uncle Victor had since moved to 163rd street. My uncle was the super of the apartment building where he lived. It was a nice apartment in the basement along with his wife and their new big dog called Lucky. The dog didn't trust me, and neither did his wife after hearing about some of the things I had done. My uncle showed me around and told me where everything was. Then he took me into the farthest part of the basement. He led me to a room, gave me a key, and told me it would be my room. He informed me what time breakfast, lunch, and dinner got served, and if I wasn't there, they would take it that I wasn't hungry. In the room, there was a cot with sheets, a blanket, a desk and a small refrigerator. Behind the wall was a tiny room made into a shower with a tiny sink. It had a smell of mold and wet concrete. It felt cold and dreary. The moment I stepped in there I was unhappy. I looked at my uncle and thought—really? I'm sure he would've rather me be with him, but because his wife wore the pants in the house, he had no choice. I knew he felt sorry for me, but he wanted the best for me and did what he could to help me grow up to be a responsible man.

My Uncle Victor.

Here I was, ten years old being put in a rat hole to live. I was passed around like a ping-pong ball and began wondering if anyone truly cared about me. I was sure Moms loved me and wanted the best for me, but she really didn't know the feelings of abandonment I experienced. Her intentions were good, and I'm sure she just wanted to protect me from Pops. I saw it in her eyes when I left that she was hurting every time she had to send me away. I loved her so much, and I didn't want to hurt her so I would never share my pain. She put me in the care of other family members and thought I was fine, but she never knew the truth of how afraid and lonely I was. As for Pops, I wondered if he ever even thought about me, or maybe he just felt hopeless because he lost control of his little boy.

At my uncle's place, my job was to go floor to floor and pick up the trash that the tenants left outside their door. I would start at the top floor every night at 8pm with my burlap sacks and work my way down to the lobby using the stairs. From the lobby, I took the elevator to the basement to throw the trash in the dumpster. Those burlap sacks got heavy. I didn't understand why I couldn't take the elevator down every floor till I reached the basement, but my uncle told me I couldn't hold the elevator up for the residents. After one day of training, I was on my own.

No Regrets

My room in the basement.

Every night I laid in bed and stared at the ceiling, listening to the sound of the elevator going up and down, the whistle of the steam pipes overhead, and the skitter of mice running around - which had always terrified me. I would crawl up to a corner in the bed with my arms across my chest frightened. Sometimes, I was afraid to move when the shadows on the wall looked like people were in the room—there were fuckin ghosts there. Most nights I'd wander up and down Broadway till I got tired enough to go to sleep without fear of the walls closing in on me. When breakfast time came, my aunt would serve me tiny portions, if I got any breakfast at all. Often, I remained hungry. While walking the streets, although I felt humiliated, I began begging for change. I would use the money to buy a slice of pizza or a piece of cake at the store while I stole some more. I hung around the Cuban restaurants at closing hours and swept floors for a plate of food. I felt so fuckin alone, and not a soul in the world gave a damn. To get away from the misery, and before I lost my fuckin mind, at night I took to hanging out and hustling on 42nd street where no one slept and the streets were always alive. I would stand around by the storefront where they sold hot dogs, hamburgers and Orange Julius directly out the window opening and beg for money to eat a frank. One time, an older Chinese man came by and offered me twenty bucks so he could take me to the park and play with my pecker for ten minutes. I was desperate and didn't know what to do, but I had to survive. I'd take the money first and stand there in disgust, asking myself, "What the fuck am I doing? What have I come to?" Then, I would take off with the money, leaving him there on his knees. After I got to know some of the other kids, when these men would approach us, we'd follow them into the park, and rob them. From there, a crew of us would sneak on the train and head over to the fountain in Central Park, party a little, then crash out on the lawn to sleep. This became my routine with the other kids out there who took me in as one of their own.

Soon, my parents got an apartment in the same building where I lived in the basement on 163rd Street and Fort Washington. It was a two-bedroom apartment. It was my brother Ed, my sisters Dee and Cindy, myself, and my mom and dad. It was a very small apartment. I was just happy to be out of that basement. I slept in the living room which was the closest to my parent's room. At times, I thought it was so Pop could keep a better eye on me. We couldn't talk, laugh, or anything else without him hearing and fussing. My uncle went back to his nightly duties of mopping and picking up garbage. I loved my uncle; he taught me many things. He would often take me fishing at City Island in the Bronx. I think sometimes it was to get me away from my dad. He taught me how to hook a worm, and got excited when I caught my first fish. Even though I didn't work for him anymore, he still gave me money. He was my mom's younger brother and they were very close. He even got a leave from the military just to be there when I was born. My parents named me after him, and he looked out for me more than he did my other siblings. I have a lot of fond memories of him.

Living back with my parents was worse than being in prison. I had a curfew and got treated like a little kid all over again. I was suffocating.

CHAPTER 3

The Pact

Revisiting the alley where the pact was made.

t was during the graffiti era that I first met Harry. I was on 163rd Street with some of the guys, and as he came walking by we both looked at each other and said, "What up?"

I said, "My name is Pepe, what's yours?"

He said, "I'm Harry."

We shook hands and from that moment on, we hung out almost every day. We never talked about our family affairs, or our pain and suffering. It took a long time to learn the reason why we just bonded; some things were better left unsaid, but we immediately felt connected. Our lives and experiences were reflected in one another. Everywhere he went, there I was. We did everything together, went everywhere together and soon, people got to know me outside of 163rd Street.

He was cool and funny at the same time. He walked with a confidence about himself which attracted me. Everywhere he went people knew him. He was easy to talk to and everyone liked him. I enjoyed hanging with him and couldn't wait till he came around. Many of the guys I hung with got jealous every time he showed up because they knew I would go off with him.

During that time period, graffiti was the big thing. Harry would scoop me up on 163rd and we'd begin our way uptown to 169th Street in the school yard of PS129. He was getting heavy into tagging with a bunch of guys. I'd done some myself, but while I was out chasing girls, these guys got hardcore, going to train yards and looking for impossible places to tag their names. Henry decided to join the United Graffiti Association (UGA), and then took it to another level by developing graffiti into an art. Murals were showing up all over, and they started to even sell paintings. Some very talented artists recognized even today came from that era. It became a movement, and another way to keep us off the streets.

I never trusted anyone at first sight. It had always been difficult for me to do so, but with Harry, I felt his sincerity, and I let my guard down. If I was hungry, we would buy a slice of pizza and split it in half. We did this

Me at 13.

with everything. We always had each other's back. One day while smoking a joint in the alleyway on 163rd, we made a pact. We promised we would never leave each other's side and always look out for one another, no matter what. When someone is willing to give his life for you, that is love. From that moment on, we became tight—we became brothers.

I got registered at Junior High School PS 143. I hated school and did anything to get out of class. I would ask for a pass to go to the bathroom two or three times every period and would stay there, along with a bunch of other kids, until someone came looking for us. No matter what I'd do, I kept getting into trouble. I really didn't see anything wrong with my behavior, but it seemed everyone had a problem with it, except me. Once we beat up the subway elevator guy on the 182nd Street 1 train because he was being a dick with us, and we all got arrested. At the courthouse we tried speaking to one another so we could get our story straight, but our families did not allow us to talk. The judge found us guilty on a misdemeanor and released us on probation with the condition that we stay away from that station and avoid all contact with the guy. This made it difficult, because it was the closest station to the school.

Harry and Herb smoking.

By this time, school was pretty much non-existent. I only showed up for homeroom just to check in because those were the conditions of my probation. Harry and the boys hung around the school waiting for me to come out so we could hang. When we got chased by truant-officers or police, we would take off to the subways and start tagging. The 168th Street tunnel was where everyone met up who cut class. Kids from Junior High School 143, Junior High School 52, Edward W. Stitt, George Washington High, Kennedy High, and others used to hang there. It seemed like everyone hated school because there was always a pretty big crowd that would show up. It usually was the same people so everyone pretty much knew each other. And the girls, well, they just loved hanging out with a bunch of crazy guys.

29

When the police chased us from there, we would head to the pool hall at Van Cortlandt in the Bronx. Fighting at the pool hall was a regular occurrence and became recreation for us. Harry was the leader and, for the most part, a serious guy with a mean streak in him. I thought he was daring and a bit crazy, and in some sick way, I was attracted to that. Besides, people respected him and I wanted that.

Coming back from the pool hall, on the train we were with some of the girls joking and laughing, jumping in and out of the subway doors before they closed. To impress them, while we were on the 238th Street station, I jumped out before the doors closed, and the train began moving, I saw the conductor stick his head in, my friend White Mike and I jumped on the little wedge at the bottom of the door and hung on the top, riding it. I laughed at the girls as I rode the train while attempting to tag my name. It was a cold, snowy day. As I let go with one hand to begin tagging, my foot slipped and, I ended up falling between the moving train and the platform. I was in shock as I held on for dear life to the train and the platform so I wouldn't get pulled under the train. My body scraped along the platform as it tore away my clothes while it continued moving. Fear overcame me. I looked up, saw the end of the platform and visualized my head running into the light pole as the train got closer. Many cars had already passed that point and my life flashed before my eyes. I knew I was going to die but I continued hanging on, praying the train would stop as the end kept getting closer. Quickly I thought, what would be the easiest death—letting go and sinking under the train wheels to be mangled to shreds, or smashing into the pole falling down to the avenue while cars below ran me over.

The girls were screaming for someone to pull the emergency brakes. Just before the end of the platform, the train came to an abrupt stop. My legs turned one way, and my torso turned the other way causing more damage. I knew for sure I had lost my legs. With my arms bleeding and skin peeled almost to the bone, I was able to crawl out with the help of my friend, White Mike, who was also tag-riding on the next train car behind me. He was terrified but helped me out just before I let go and fell under. As I laid there naked I could see through the closed doors window the look on the girls faces—they were horrified as I screamed in agony. White Mike used his new cashmere coat to cover me while I waited for the ambulance. I was cold and the blood oozing from my legs made it worst. I laid there in agony for what seemed like forever, until the ambulance arrived. When they got there, they treated what they could and then put me on the stretcher. Going down the stairs with all the bouncing, was very painful.

I was rushed to Columbia Presbyterian Hospital. I broke some bones and tore eighty percent of the muscles in my legs. God was with me. The doctors said I may not ever get full feeling back, but with therapy, I would improve and possibly walk again. One bad decision and just like that, in a flash of a minute my life was drastically changed. This was one of the scariest moments of my life. My legs were completely numbed. I continued touching them for any sensation. I became depressed and was down on myself. Many negative thoughts raced through my mind. I wanted to die. I could not see myself in a wheelchair. Often, I would beat on my legs without feeling anything and cry. It was a tough period. I had to make a decision quickly before depression took me over. I became determined to walk again. I was staying at my brother Jimbo's house again. He moved around the corner from my parents in uptown Manhattan. Every day my mom came to see me. She would massage my legs and, never stopped encouraging me, telling me not to give up because I am going to walk in the name of God. She would help me get out of the wheelchair and onto my crutches to practice walking.

My injury didn't stop the guys from hanging in my house and partying during school hours while my brother was at work. Whenever they'd come over, I'd have a bag on my lap, and they would all drop in some weed. It carried me through the times when I was alone.

Through many months of rehabilitation and God's will, I was able to walk again. I called my mom on the phone one day and began screaming her name. She rushed over and found me on the living room floor crying. She asked me what happened. I looked up and told her, "I took a few steps without my crutches."

Mom helped me to my feet, and we cried together. From that point on, I knew I would walk again. The sensation in my legs crept back, and little by little, I began to use the wheelchair less. I pushed myself hard every day. I walked with my crutches in the hallway and held onto the stair railing to go up and down the stairs. The day came when I no longer needed crutches. From then on, I walked everywhere no matter how far or how long it took me. The trains were pretty much a joke to us. We used them for recreation, riding between the cars, riding on top of them, on the doors, and for graffiti. Guys were dying, but that didn't faze us. Until that day, when I stared death in the face, I developed a new respect for it. It was a long time before I rode the subway again and when I did, I always took a giant step over the platform into the train for fear I would fall to the tracks below. That was the dumbest thing I had ever done, and the last time I ever attempted anything like it again.

CHAPTER 4

The Gangs

The seventies was a time of political and cultural change in America. Movements like the Black Panthers and the Young Lords were big. Youth immigrants were coming from other countries, many barrio kids came from broken homes left unsupervised or with poor guidance, and even the Puerto Ricans who felt left behind by a failed system, all took to the streets and found refuge by joining gangs. Being a gang member meant brotherhood and protection. Not all groups were bad. Some gangs even served to protect and help the community from drug dealing in hallways, or on the block when kids came home from school. We were all looking to connect with one another and feel the love that some of us didn't get at home. It gave us a sense of social acceptance and pride.

By this time, no school wanted me except Jr. High School PS 52. I joined a gang called the Red Devils, and soon after, got kicked out from that school as well. Because of my age, I got skipped up and made it to George Washington High School, where I only attended to hang out and eat Sloppy Joes during lunch hour. As soon as I hit sixteen, against my mom's wishes and cries, I planned to get her to sign me out of school.

Harry became a member of a gang called the Latin Demons. I had a hard time getting in because of my young age. I had to do a few things to prove myself. With Harry's pushing, eventually I did. I was thrilled when I got my colors and became a Demon. Harry had already become the Warlord. We were less like a gang and more like a social club. We smoked weed, drank beer and hung out. It was all about the girls and our newly decorated basement club house with the red and blue lights playing the slow jams and dancing with the girls who loved to hang around us.

Our clubhouse was the spot. Everyone heard about it and wanted to come by and see what was going on. We all pitched in and helped to beautify it by painting, cleaning, and getting whatever furniture we could find. We put glowing fluorescent posters up on every wall so that when the blue light would hit them, they would light up, as did our teeth and any white color clothing. Yeah, the lights were special. There was something about those red and blue lights, and the darkness, that made us feel good.

Danny, one of our gang members, was an artist, and he designed the Demon logo for our colors, which we wore with our club name on the back of a cut-sleeve Lee jean jacket. He also painted the same thing on a wall all by itself, which for many nights we would just look at and admire.

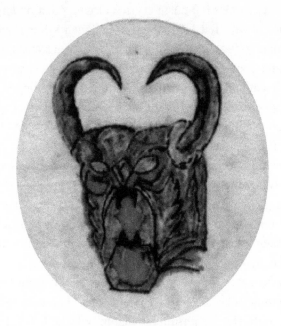

The Latin Demons Logo.

Those who wanted to get their groove on with a girl would go to another part of the basement on the hush hush. At times, there would be two or three couples making out there while the more serious stuff was in the darkest spot where no light existed. There wasn't a whole lot of conversations going on as we lounged out, listening to music, dancing, or watching others dance, while we puffed on a joint or drank beer. It was like we were frozen in time. No one wanted to go out into the daylight, so we'd stay down there forever.

Every group or gang on the West side did the same. There were the Saints on 134th street, the Falcons on 160th, Galaxies on 163rd, us on 164th, the Blue Demons on 170th, the Brother Galaxies uptown, and The Knights, along with one or two more. The East side in Spanish Harlem had the Vice-roys, Hell's Kitchen in Manhattan had the Westies, an Irish gang, then you had the Italians. Brooklyn had the Dirty Ones, among others. The Bronx, our neighboring borough, had the same, only on a larger scale. They had 153 gangs plus motorcycle clubs—the Bronx was wilding. Even today there are some that survived and are still out there, like the Savage Nomads, the Savage Skulls, the Black Spades, and the Chingalings, who now own the entire building on Hughes Avenue in the Crotona section. It was all innocent at first—the "in" thing, a way for us to be off the streets and have a sense of ownership. It was where we met and socialized before all the madness which was to come later.

Our club meetings were members only. We'd talk about issues, new members, duties, and we collected regular dues to pay the super his rent and for our club expenses or whatever came up. Nobody minded putting in their fair share because we had the baddest club of all, which made others jealous. Afterwards we'd hang around, clean up, play cards, tell jokes and laugh a lot. We were happy there, like brothers united, having a lot of fun with a sense of pride and belonging. We were in heaven and nothing else mattered. Needless to say that my childhood girlfriend Terry and I began to see each other less and less.

A group of us used to go to Delancey and haggle for clothes. It was the time of the Playboy shoes, the knits, alpacas, sharkskin silk pants, beaver hats, and cashmere coats. It was the lover's period. The time of groups like the Delfonics, The Moments, The Dells, The Whatnots, Blood Stone and Peaches & Herb. We went to all of the Catholic school dances at Mother Cabrini, Incarnation, St. Rose of Lima, and Sacred Heart of Mary, to grind and do the 500 with the girls (when we go way down with our thigh up their crotch). Couples would make out behind the bleachers, in the bathrooms or outside. We would huddle around to make cover so we could take turns with our girls and the nuns wouldn't be able to see. When the party ended, and the lights came on, the nuns were always shocked. We were a bunch of horny teenagers looking for more action. We had to cover our erections whenever we left the dance. Those were the good old days when we were somewhat innocent.

Breaking into cars and stores had become the norm. My friends and I got caught breaking into a fruit and vegetable stand on Broadway just for fun once. We had a food fight and made a mess of the place. We walked into the 34th Precinct with stains from the fruit and vegetables all over us. My mother had to collect me. She didn't tell Pop anything. I knew she was disappointed in me because she slapped me across the face in front of my friends and the police. The cops all smiled; it seemed like they got a kick out of that.

When I went before the judge, he sentenced me to Spofford Juvenile Detention. After a while, I was given an alternative to the detention center. I could go to jail or go into a group home. I chose the group home. I was sent to a home on St. Laurence, in the Bronx. I was on my best behavior while there. I earned a leave and was able to go home for a visit.

It was during this time that I met my new girlfriend Andrea when I was out on a pass from the group home. She was pretty, and appeared to be the most popular girl on the block. I was fourteen, she was seventeen and had a little son. I wasn't sure what she saw in a loser like me, besides my good looks. I had nothing to offer and my life was going nowhere. I had no goals, no ambition and deep down inside, I felt I would end up with nothing because I was always looking for the easy way out. Now, here's this older girl taking an interest in me, so I decided to go for the ride, and I ended up leaving my girl Terry for her. I wouldn't have left Terry, but because this new girl was jealous, she told me I had to choose one of them.

Being the only Spanish kid in the group home, I felt a little uncomfortable. We would go out as a group to the movies, ball games, and other places. I didn't connect with anyone there. I felt too grown to hang out with these kids. Most of them were younger than me. The ones that were my age were square and not in my league. Everywhere we went I tried hard not to be seen with them because I was embarrassed. I didn't care to participate in any of the outings. I felt locked up there, and soon I began breaking the rules. I would involve the others to sneak out at night and climb over a fence to go night swimming or hang out. I started bringing in weed and got everyone high, even the young ones that never smoked weed before. The staff learned what was going on because one of the kids snitched on me. My room got searched, and I was called in for questioning. I denied everything. A new kid came in and began doing the same things as me. Things got out of control.

Entrance to the Latin Demons' Basement.

I was tired of being accused for everyone else's doing, and after some months, I decided to escape. In the middle of the night, I tied some sheets together and climbed out the second-floor window. I went back home to see my girl and hang out with my friends. The police caught me at a relative's house, and I got remanded to Spofford Juvenile Detention to await my next court date. When I went before the judge again, my mother was there. She pleaded with the judge, and he placed me in her custody.

By the time I got back to the block, Harry had already been with his girl for some time. They were the most popular couple in town. Everywhere he went there she was. She was a tough chick and a member of the Hell-La-

Fy Sisters, a chapter from the Savage Nomads gang. They were one of the biggest gangs in the Bronx. We really had no issues with any gangs, other than the Black Spades, who had caught Harry in the Bronx with his colors and beat him down. At that time, everyone respected each other's territory and tried not to wear colors outside their turf. Nevertheless, they still attacked one of us, and we had to get revenge. We were always going to the Bronx to search for Black Spades. It had nothing to do with being black, because we too were a mixed bunch, but it was all about the principle—it was always about principle! Whenever we found a Spade, we beat them down and took their colors. Later, though, some of us became friends.

Jew Park became another hangout spot. We called it Jew Park because at that time, only Jewish people lived around there, and the actual park name, no one could remember. It was on 173rd and Fort Washington near the George Washington Bridge, right by the A train. There were Hasidic Jews with the beanie caps and long sideburns. We were fine living together and sometimes we'd even protect them from getting messed with or robbed. But, we were a loud and intimidating bunch, and, little by little, the sweet, easy-going families stopped visiting the park. We took control of the park. No one got through that park if we didn't want them to. You had to be peaceful and respect our turf. We sat on each side of the wall entrance sometimes smoking weed, controlling all movement in and out of the park, as if we were the gatekeepers. At the back of the park, you can get a really nice view of the George Washington Bridge, and at night, that's where we hung out, looking at the bright lights in amusement. Those were some good memories.

My girl Andrea and I got tight. She came out pregnant so I pleaded with my mom to let us stay at the house for a little while. She was very hesitant because of my dad, and she needed to talk it over with him. My parents really didn't like her. They thought she was too old for me, and it was too soon to have a baby because we barely knew one another. My mom tried talking with me about my decisions, but I didn't want to hear it. They finally let us stay at the house, with conditions and only for a brief while.

With the help of her uncle, we got our first apartment. She supported the household, and we ate with her food stamps and she even bought my first pair of Mush Melos shoes with her welfare check. Just about every day we would eat corned beef with white rice or Chef Boyardee Spaghetti in the can. I began to look like a spaghetti noodle, but I didn't complain. It was much better than the many nights I had nothing to eat at all. Now, I felt like I was living large. She took me in as a hard core precocious child and led me into my manhood.

My youth skipped over me. While she was pregnant, I had to act like a man, and help raise her first born son who was only two years old. Playing Ring-o-Levio, Johnny-on-the-Pony, Kick-the-Can, and stick-ball, only happened when my girl wasn't around. She said, "Only kids played that" and that "I had to be a man now." She was good to me. We made do with what we had, and I had my little hustle selling loose joints for a buck each.

Our house became the other hangout spot. We smoked, snorted, drank, played cards and listened to music. Every day was exciting, and just about every weekend my clothes were flying out the window. It became the joke among the crew. When that woman opened her mouth to yell my name out the window, the boys would say, "Oh oh, there goes your clothes again." We had a lot of love for one another, but no communication skills. There was always some drama going down. I was always quick to react to things without thinking first, and she was a no-nonsense person who was very fast to the draw. When Andrea yelled, all hell would break loose. When my anger rose, I wouldn't know how to react except to go on the offense cursing. It was a dysfunctional relationship to say the least.

I never put my hands on her, but there were many times I wanted to in order to shut her big mouth. It was difficult for me to explain myself so I would become frustrated. I would punch the walls when I had enough of her crap, or I would grab her hard by her arms and shake her when she wouldn't stop.

The responsibility of being a man when I was just a boy weighed heavy on me. It wasn't long before we would be broken up behind some false accusation. I went over to Mick's girlfriend for a free haircut. She was a student hairdresser and needed practice, so she used me for more experience, and I got a free haircut. It was nothing more. All the guys knew where I went. When I got back home, I knew something was wrong. Everyone was silent. I approached Andrea, and she had this look in her face that could kill. She told me to find another place to live because it was over. I begged her and told her nothing happened. I asked her to please believe me, but no matter what I said it didn't matter. My clothes were once again flying out the window. Mick didn't want to hear it either, so I walked away. I picked up what little of the clothes I could and headed back to mom's house. It didn't matter because it was over anyways. That was the first time I regretted not doing someone's girl because I got blamed anyway.

A few days later I went to a party at The Knights' club, and I saw Andrea there dancing with Mick's brother Joey. She was using Joey to get back at me. I looked up and saw Joey grinding to a slow jam and making out with her. I pulled out my 007 knife to stab him; he saw me coming and caused a lot of commotion. The Knights didn't take it as a sign of aggression, especially since it was not with one of their guys. Besides, they knew who she was and her relation to me. They respected that, but didn't allow fighting in the club. They took me outside and asked me to leave—I was livid. The pain from what I witnessed filled my mind with thoughts of revenge. I couldn't comprehend how she could act that way especially while carrying my baby. That night I went to Joey's house near Jew Park armed with my knife, ready to stab the shit out of him.

As I was approaching, I saw them getting out of a cab together. I began moving forward with the knife in my hand. He noticed me and began to move faster through the long walkway into the building. I tried lunging at him with the knife; he used my girl Andrea like a shield as she began screaming. He said, "I swear Pepe, nothing happened. It's over." He went into the building while she remained there with me. I called her a bunch of names and left her there crying. I went back to my mom's place.

Pop was very uncomfortable to have me back. The next day I walked onto 163rd Street and saw Joey there playing Chinese handball. I stepped to him. He kept apologizing saying, "Nothing happened" and that it was over. I made a fist and punched him in the face. We fought for a hot three minutes and he kicked my ass. Not only was I hurt physically, but also emotionally. I was humiliated! The trust was gone and this crushed me.

Eventually, we moved on, and with time, that was that. As for Mick, he just always believed I slept with his girl, so that changed our relationship forever. My girl and I continued to go back and forth; however, I was never faithful after that. I loved her, and she did me wrong. My heart was broken, and by this time I had grown cold. I became cruel and careless.

No Regrets

I became tired of the same shit over and over again. I knew I wasn't happy, but by this time she had given birth to my son Anthony, and even though I was proud to be a father, now I felt stuck. I loved my son, he was the most handsome baby ever—just like his dad. I was proud of him, and I tolerated plenty of crap to stay by his side. But I knew that one day I'd be gone forever, and the thought of leaving him was affecting me.

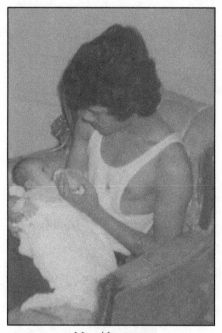

Me with my son.

Once, she took a knife and chased me around my son's crib to stab me. When she trapped me, instead of stabbing me, she ended up cutting herself and off to the hospital we went. It was a break-up to make-up relationship. This all started wrong. If only I had been wise enough to notice the signs earlier, or listen to my mom when she tried telling me I was making a mistake.

One night out of the blue, our clubhouse got violated. Someone had broken into our only safe haven, our clubhouse and wrecked the place. The furniture was broken, the sofas were all slashed, and paint had been thrown all over the beautiful Demon logo we were all so proud of. Underneath our logo was the name "The Knights." It totally threw us off because The Knights were cool with us. Although the bond wasn't thick, we had peace with them. Some of us were friends. I saw them every day on my way home because my parents now lived down the street from them. They had a beautiful basement clubhouse on the corner of Audubon Avenue. We frequently visited each other's clubhouse when we had parties. We were shocked, angry, and confused. The issue with The Knights grew, and the very next day we decided to get revenge. We couldn't comprehend how they could do this to us. We partied, laughed, danced and drank with them and this is what they do behind our back. We never expected this.

A Latin Demons tag on the 168ᵗʰ street subway stop.

Will, the President of the Latin Demons declared war, and Nick, the Vice President, decided it was time to move, and Harry took the lead. We wanted an explanation for why they would break into and vandalize our clubhouse, especially when we thought we were cool with them.

We armed ourselves with knives, bats, and zip guns and headed uptown in separate groups. It was early afternoon. We walked on Amsterdam Avenue where there were plenty of grocery stores, restaurants and people so that we would blend in and not attract attention. Then, we all met up at a nearby park to regroup so that we'd look large when we went to The Knights.

No Regrets

The landscape in the Heights was pretty much all the same; five to six story buildings all joined together and most either had an alley with a ramp or stairs with rails or gates going downstairs to the basement in the front of the building. The basements were large with many rooms where the super usually lived, kept tools, stored the trash, or rented rooms. Many clubhouse rooms were rented to us by the supers on the down low without the owner knowing, as long as we kept our cool and took off when the landlord was coming. We used these alley stairs to enter the basement clubhouses. We turned the corner onto the block where their clubhouse was located. We were all very serious and quiet. The look on everyone's face was stoned, mixed with anger and fear. I felt the fear and anxiety. This was the very first time as a group we'd gone to war. These guys were bigger and older than us. They were more organized and I'm sure they had weapons, unlike the little crappy stuff we had. I was apprehensive and scared. I was hoping these guys were not there and we could just wreck their place and leave quickly without incident. We crossed the street, and most of us were now at the tip of the stairs ready to go down into their club, while some of us stood on the sidewalk keeping guard so we wouldn't be ambushed. Just as we began rushing down the long stairway, some of their guys were coming out. When they saw us, they had this surprised look on their faces. At about three steps before the bottom level, they tried stopping us, yelling loudly and preventing us from going further. We surprised them; they clearly didn't know what was going on.

We asked, "What happened to our clubhouse?" as we pushed forward. We were all yelling at the same time; we outnumbered the four to five men they had. They weren't able to stop us as we kept pushing our way through. Someone threw a punch and a full-on brawl broke out, and when one of them pulled out a knife, Harry took out his dagger in response and stabbed his attacker. I heard the scream and we all froze at the same time. All the fighting stopped. It was a sound I'd never heard before as we watched the guy drop to the ground. Blood splattered everywhere. The guys closest to him had blood on their faces and all over their clothing.

We all stood there in total shock as we saw the guy take his last gasp of air, his body jerked, and then he laid motionless. We watched his friends come to assist him, cradling his head and screaming his name. We all scattered out of there. We ran, then walked fast in groups back onto the avenue the way we came, in total silence again with fear freshly painted on our faces. Everyone was scared. Some went home, while others decided it was better to stick together and hide on a rooftop on 161st Street. We waited there for hours and watched all the movement below. That night, The Knights took to patrolling our block in long military-like trench coats. Everyone knew when more than one guy wore the trench, they were packing something big underneath. Fear was in the air.

Being a member of the Latin Demons made it difficult for me to get home every day since I lived in The Knights' territory. I had to take the long way around, go through alleyways, and climb over rooftops every time to avoid The Knights, but that didn't last long. There came a time when everywhere we went we would run into one of them. Many fights took place. Fights broke out on Broadway, coming out of the San Juan Theater at the Audubon Ballroom where Malcolm X was killed, or at Jew park. Sometimes we would match up fighters and then watch each other go at it. Things progressed from fistfights to knives, then to guns. Things were getting out of control and definitely out of the scope of who we were. It wasn't about violence for us; we were just teens trying to have one another's back and look out for each other so we could have a good time at our clubhouse.

This was not the way we had envisioned things. Although we had gone up there prepared for a fight, we weren't prepared for what had actually happened with the stabbing. We had knives and other weapons, but in our minds they were just for protection. As a group, we didn't even own a gun. The stabbing was never meant to happen. It was self-defense.

After that, everything changed. Many of the guys moved out to different places; Pennsylvania, Poconos, upstate New York and various boroughs, while others joined the military. Those that stayed got arrested but were later released because we were minors. No one talked or snitched to the police. Everyone became tired of the fighting after a while. Eventually, the animosity between us on the street lost its presence.

But, the stabbing incident had a profound impact on all our lives. No one was ever the same again. Without a shadow of a doubt, we all accepted that a mistake was made. We knew nothing would ever be the same. None of us had ever experienced anything of such nature or even close. The fear of the unknown created a deafening silence, and most of us carried a heavy heart.

For Harry, it hit the hardest. I saw how that incident had changed him the most. Years later, he went back to that same location to light a candle for the deceased. We eventually lost our clubhouse, and that alone was devastating. We knew it was the end of an era. We no longer had a place to call our own and unite other than Jew park. The good times ended for us as a group and many of us couldn't get used to that. Others were just afraid to go back, in fear of being an easy target for The Knights. It was no longer a safe place for us. Everything was gone now, in just the blink of an eye.

One day, some of us took the risk and went back there for the last time, as we stood there in disbelief, totally silent, with broken hearts and wanting to cry. I remember being resistant, saying "We don't have to give the club up, we can fix it up better than before, and if they come here, we'll put up a fight." While the others felt my sentiment, they thought I was crazy, and knew the danger it could put us in. I guess it was true, we really weren't a gang, and it wasn't worth someone else dying. I was mad, and even attempted to call some of the guys punks, wanting them to reason with me, but I saw the sadness and fear in their faces and decided to ease off. As hard as it was, it was time to let go and move on. For most of us, this was a very tough call, as our world turned upside down by this one totally unexpected event and, as much as we wanted to stay together even without a club, we knew deep within that "The Latin Demons" would be no longer. And for our very own protection, we had no choice but to join forces with the biggest gang in the hood called, The Galaxies. It's what they were always after, as we soon found out.

The Galaxies were a predominantly Dominican gang from the upper West Side and directly around the corner from us. Many of our guys were unhappy and resisted joining them. Although many of us were friends, we just didn't like or trust them. They always seemed to show up when we least expected them, and that made some of us uncomfortable. The Demons that joined them did so grudgingly. Now we were known as "The Young Galaxies."

Months later we learned the Galaxies had planned this all along. They were the ones who had broken into our clubhouse so that we would go to war with their rivals, The Knights. It was all a part of their plan to co-opt us. They had a clue that we knew something, but never said anything. Many of us got disgusted with this and walked away from The Galaxies. Some of us talked about getting even. However, we were all drained. We didn't have enough guys left for a power move against them. Those that were around wanted no part of it. An innocent guy already died over some nonsense. Enough blood was shed. It was a bitter pill to swallow, but we accepted it and moved on. No one ever talked about it again. It was an experience that shaped our lives, and now it got pushed back into the farthest part of our memory bank. Everyone went in different directions. Harry and Joey enlisted in the Marines. Some got caught up in selling or using drugs in a big way. By now, against Mom's protest, I had been signed out of school, and was waiting until my seventeenth birthday to enlist in the Marines and following my brothers who joined the army

My baby's mom and I finally broke up. I was done with all the arguing and moved back to my parents' house. This time I was sure it was over for good, and I began dating someone new. When she got wind of it—even though we were not together—she took it as I cheated on her, and all hell would break loose again with more drama that would last for weeks. I continued hanging out on the block where she lived across from the old clubhouse. I couldn't be away from my son for too long so I was always over there. Everywhere I went I took him with me, even if only to chill downstairs while she did her thing. I could always be seen looking in the direction of our old clubhouse, reminiscing on all those good old times with the Demons.

When my old friend Joey returned home from boot camp, we talked and cleared the air about my baby mama—now ex-girl. All was forgiven and we started hanging together. The guys found Joey arrogant, but the girls loved him. He was tall, handsome, smart, muscular, a sharp dresser, and very cocky. Joey was exciting, brave, spontaneous and full of great ideas. He was studying to be a hairstylist. We started sticking people up in underground parking garages in Queens. Every other week we had a new stolen Cadillac. Then we began planning to stick up hair salons he knew. I thought, maybe he got fired from there, or he never got hired, or maybe got a bad haircut. Whatever it was, I didn't ask or care.

No Regrets

My friend Harry in his Marine uniform.

It was the Disco era. That was all people were talking about, "This club, that club, this club that." Clubs were opening up all over the place, from disco to freestyle to salsa at the Epoca, the Corso or Club Broadway. It was all about getting dressed, putting on the best cologne and feeling like you were John Travolta in Saturday Night Fever. When you made that entrance, you wanted everyone to notice. Once you heard the music, your insides came alive and your feet and hands started tapping to the beat, letting go of whatever bad times or thoughts you were having. It was like food for the soul and being in heaven. The women did their own thing, trying to outdo each other for the best dressed as they strutted back and forth to be seen. It was like the Oscars contest for best dancer in full glamour.

Five to six days a week we did a little toot then headed to the Bronx to the Hunts Point Palace, the Stardust Ballroom or, midtown to the clubs where all the action was at the heartbeat of New York City, where all nations came together to enjoy the Broadway theaters, the restaurants, the garment district, or shop at the largest diamond district in the world—where the city lights shine bright throughout the night. Ipanema, Roseland, The Grand Ballroom, Contiki Lounge, Red Parrot, Ruby Fruit, The Ice Palace, Studio

54, The Tunnel or the Copa were some of the hottest clubs in NYC. Things were popping, and we were living it up. Joey was dating one of the Latin Symbolic dancers at the Ipanema. Not only was the Ipanema our favorite spot, but sometimes we got in free, and we were able to sit at a table without being harassed by the waiters trying to sell us more drinks, plus Roseland Ballroom was directly across the street on 52nd street, Boom Bamako on Broadway, the Con Tiki, Studio 54 and most of the other clubs were all within walking distance. We hopped back and forth on any given night. It was always alive—the atmosphere was electrifying.

The Hustle dance, and Freestyle were big, then Hip Hop started coming into the picture. When I got onto the dance floor, I was in another world. I freaked out and I felt free, without a care in the world and nothing else mattered but the feeling of that moment. Everyone did their own thing and no one judged you, and if they did, I didn't give a shit. It was about spacing out and de-stressing. Everyone from Manhattan, Brooklyn to the Bronx was partying—it was all about the clubs, the girls and having fun.

My relationship with Joey grew stronger. Together, we got a furnished room on 187th Street off Audubon and moved in. We were making money, rolling up to the clubs in newly stolen cars, dressing fly and, picking up a lot of women. Our small furnished room uptown, in the Heights, was always busy. Sometimes he used the main bed, and I was on the floor or vice versa. The girls didn't care.

While at this house party in the Bronx one night, some stick-up kids came in and robbed the entire party. They took our money, jewelry, and coats with our guns in them. We were pissed. I mean, how could they have done this to us? We were the stick-up kids. We walked out into the cold, late night with no money and a long way back home. We were so mad and cold that we began walking without talking. The few drinks we had were holding us up as we thought about how to make it from the Bronx to the Heights. A drunk man stumbled out of a car into a building in front of us. We looked at each other and instantly knew this was our opportunity. We moved quickly behind him before the door shut. We grabbed and wrestled him to the ground. As we struggled with the man, he tried to reach for something. We noticed he had a gun. We were able to take it from him and began beating him with it. We searched his pockets and found a badge. The guy was a cop.

CHAPTER 5

Gladiator School

Joey and I were scared of getting caught with a badge, so we decided to get rid of it. I wiped off our fingerprints from it then threw it in a trash can along the sidewalk. We kept the gun because guns didn't come easy and besides, we needed it. Life went on as usual, the partying, getting high and the women. We were living the dream, or so we thought. One night, while Joey was sleeping on the bed with his date and me on the floor with mine, there was a loud knock on the door. We heard, "Police open the door." Frozen with fear, we could only look at each other in silence before the door came crashing down on top of my date and me.

I was taken to central booking and charged with the attempted murder of a police officer with robbery in the first degree. I got processed and questioned for hours. I wasn't sure why it was only me they took, but I soon learned the cop could only identify me. I don't typically mess with cops, and when I found out he was a cop, it was too late. I didn't give Joey up and got put on the next bus to Rikers Island. It was bad. I didn't know what was going to happen, but I knew I was scared as hell. If I got convicted, I was going to face a lot of time. I started bugging out. The image of my son's face kept showing up. He would surely be waiting for me to come see him. His little heart would break. Damn, I was hurting so bad. I fucked up again. The thought of being in jail was killing me. I didn't know if I could take the shit I got myself into this time.

In the bullpen, I did push-ups to get ready for what awaited me at Rikers Island. It was known as the worst jail in the country. They called it the Gladiator School. I had been there before when I was charged with a stabbing during Christmas eve of 1975, but I had been bailed out the following day. Nevertheless, I was frightened as hell, but I had to pretend not to be. I needed to put on an image of some bad guy, so I put on that mask that I was familiar with. We got to Rikers Island C-74 where all the minors are taken, and stayed in the bullpen for processing with a bunch of other cats. Some were kicking drugs, shitting and vomiting all over the place. The smell made me want to puke. I picked the furthest corner from the toilet and sat there. It was a very long night. We ate a bologna sandwich, then got directed to a back room where we got strip-searched. Afterward, we were taken to another back room and hosed down with a high-pressure hose before going for a medical. The correction officer (CO), called out our names and told us where we would be housed. Sometime in the early morning, we got led to the cell block at building 5. The whole process wore me out. At the locking house, I could hear all the chatter and catcalls from the prisoners as we walked through the cell block to the end of the corridor where my cell would be at. I kept my stare straight ahead. The fear was choking me so much; I thought I would pass out. I got put in a one-man cell. When the doors closed behind me, I put the sheet I was given in my mouth and began to cry. I was paranoid of anyone hearing, so I tried to be quiet. My world came crashing down on me and my life got turned upside down in a flash. That feeling of once again being lost returned, only this time I knew it would be there for a long time to come. The thought petrified me. Everything and everyone I loved flashed across my mind. I was hurting with a familiar pain deep in my soul. That night, I couldn't sleep.

The following day my cell door opened and I was able to take a shower. I thought that maybe I could scrub some of this pain away.

While in the shower, I heard something and looked up to notice the electric door to the shower being pried open. This guy slid-in and locked it behind him. I became tense and uncomfortable. I looked at him as he approached me with his hand tucked under a towel. My heart started racing. I knew something bad was about to go down. As he got closer, his hand came out from under the towel, I saw the shiny, sharp object. He said, "Turn around and be quiet." I stood there terrified staring at him without moving, while he kept saying, "Turn around." A flash of being molested as a boy tore through my mind and the fear and anger rose through me. "This was not going to happen again," I thought, and I waited until he got closer, and then reached for the object and held onto his hand for dear life. We wrestled to the ground. His head crashed onto the floor and I was able to take the shank from him. Before I blacked out, I had a flashback. I remembered seeing the guy's face that once molested me, I grew angry, and stabbed him over and over again. When I came to, there was blood everywhere, and he laid there motionless. I quickly rinsed off the blood, got dressed, slipped through the door and headed to my cell. I sat quietly and listened for any commotion. After a while, I heard the static. The shower door opened and he was found on the ground with the shower running. Medics came and took him away. Everyone got directed to their cells and put on lockdown. I laid on the bed waiting for that door to be open and get arrested again, only now, for murder. To my surprise, nothing happened, but I wasn't out of the woods yet. The CO had to know I was in there because the shower door closed a minute or so after I went in. Others had seen me going into the shower as well, and I'm sure someone knew what he was doing, but no one said a thing.

The next day all the cell doors opened for recreation, but I stayed in my cell. I was afraid of something happening. Crazy thoughts raced through my mind. The only time I came out that day was to eat. The following day I came out and walked to the room where they had the recreational area. I took a corner and stood there with my back against the wall keeping an eye on everything that moved, as some played cards while others watched TV. Then some guys came and introduced themselves to me. From that moment on, I began to relax. Word spread quickly through the jail. Everywhere I went people knew who I was. I had respect overnight and others knew not to fuck with me. But deep down inside, I was still scared, only now I had to play the role I took and keep wearing the mask. The more people heard about what I did, the better it was for me and the less I had to prove. My worry was that the COs would also find out. But it was pretty much us against them, and if anyone snitched in there, everyone would learn about it, and even in protective custody, no one is safe. It was the unspoken rule that all abided by -the code. I became a badass over-night. I grew more comfortable and confident by the day as I continued to wear that mask. This was the only way a young, skinny, pretty kid like me was going to survive in here.

Some days had gone by, and word came that the guy I stabbed almost died. He would probably end up paralyzed. I found out that he was a Dominican drug dealer with powerful family connections from the Heights. Apparently, because he was a big shot in the streets, he thought he could push his weight around in jail. A lot of people were afraid of him. He enjoyed sodomizing newcomers and continuously got away with it. On my way to chow one day, I received a written message that read, "Watch your back."

Because of the affiliation, a week later, my childhood friend Renzo was also charged with the same crime as me and was at another part of the jail. He had become my little sister's childhood sweetheart, and they were now married and she was some months pregnant. On our next court date, his charges were dropped due to lack of evidence. I was so happy about that. He could now care for my sister and their upcoming baby. To avoid any beef, I spent more time in my cell.

That's when I read my very first book ever at the age of seventeen. It was called *Down These Mean Streets* by Piri Thomas. I remember how inspired I felt, and looking back now, it was also when for the first time I knew that one day I would be writing my story. I then read *Run Baby Run* by Nicky Cruz. His story fascinated me. At that moment, it became clear, that I knew I had a chance and I could change. The thought of writing was always on my mind, but because of my lack of education and my grammar being weak, the thought just became a fantasy. However, that thought lingered on for as long as I can remember, but with all the obstacles in my life, it just became another useless thought. My second book was *The Greatest Salesman in The World* by Og Mandino. I was so inspired by the instructional scrolls that I found a way to make a copy in order to keep following the message so I could become successful. This book started me on my journey, it gave me hope. I began to alter my thinking, and from that point on, I tried reading self-help books. It was the first time in my life, that I knew I wanted to try changing and be better.

Most inmates identified with Piri and Nicky's stories because they were street guys. Books were scarce, so when we got a good book, we passed it around like toilet paper. Thereafter, I went on a mission to get and read all the books from these authors. They weren't easy to find, and when you did, they were like gold for those who liked to read. Other books which inspired me were, *Malcolm X, The Power of Now* by Eckhart Tolle, *Pulling Your Strings* by Dr. Wayne Dyer and *The Seat of The Soul* by Gary Zukav. These really helped me tremendously. If it weren't for these books early on, I think I would've gone insane, or probably got caught up in the jailhouse drama and be doing life. There was a shift in my thinking. I was beginning to feel something I've never felt, as though some transformation was taking place.

No Regrets

Turnover at the jail was constant. Watching the newcomers walking with that same look I did, I could feel their fear. I grew empathy for them. The inmates did what was done to them when they first walked in; it was some kind of ritual, but whenever I could, I made sure that no one messed with them. Somehow, I took on the role of their protector. By now, others throughout the jail knew my name and everyone gave me a lot of respect. But that still didn't stop all the fighting I had to do with guys that just didn't give a shit and were as miserable. The differences always occurred and there was no love lost. Everything was a test or a challenge for the biggest and baddest lion to win. Plenty of times, we'd ask the CO to allow us a one-on-one. They didn't care if we killed each other, besides, they enjoyed watching fights, it was something to break their boredom. I fought with a lot of anger and no fight was ever clean; some I won and some I didn't, but I proved my point—you were going to know someone was standing before you, and that alone caused anyone to think twice about trying to push up on me. Not much went down without my knowledge. I was somewhat of a shot caller where I housed. Some COs still gave me a hard time when they read why I was there. Often they would introduce me as "the cop beater." I had to learn the ropes fast to be able to survive. But the Mask never came off.

Everyone hung out in the recreation room and watched the new guys come in. One day, I did a double take cause I couldn't believe my eyes. It was Joey. I yelled his name. When he looked up and saw me, he smiled. I couldn't wait for him to get to his cell so we could catch up. I told the CO he was my brother and he allowed me to see him. I ran to where he was and hugged him. He told me he got arrested doing some stuff to try and bail me out. I couldn't have been happier to see my boy here with me instead of elsewhere in the jail. I pulled some strings to get a two-man cell and got Joey placed with me. Suddenly doing time became a little easier. We played chess, Casino, Spades, told stories and reminisced about the past.

Joey got diesel working out. Everyone in the jail knew he was like my brother, so if you messed with one you messed with the other. It gave us more power and he was a good fighter. After being together a year, Joey's case came up. He was sentenced and sent upstate. Although I was happy for him getting out of this shit hole, once again I felt that loneliness, and the familiar feeling of being alone and abandoned swept over me.

Doing time suddenly became hard again. I had a plan to escape from the island if I didn't win my case. During recreation every day, a few of us would take turns, opening a broken cell that no one lived in as others watched, and with some metal we tried to chip away at the wall to plan our escape. Four months later, I blew trial on a lesser charge. At the following court date, I got sentenced to eight years, plus another three years to run concurrent from that 1975 stabbing, which I was out on bail from. I felt defeated. I was emotionally, spiritually and physically drained from the month-long trial and I had no fight left in me. I was just in need for change and getting on up outta there; anything had to be better than Rikers where the days felt like months, months like years and the routine was always the same. I sort of surrendered to the system so they could do whatever they wanted with me. Because I didn't get the time I expected, I changed my mind about escaping, and within a month I was shipped upstate. After spending eighteen months at Rikers Island, aka the Gladiator School, I was happy to move on, and maybe at least see Joey again.

A big Greyhound bus was waiting to take a group of us to Elmira State Penitentiary, also known as The Big House. Throughout the whole twelve-hour ride, I had knots in my belly. Although better than the 12 ½-15 years I was expecting for the bigger charges, the fear of spending the next eight years of my life behind those walls was overwhelming. It seemed like a lifetime with no end. I just couldn't bear the thought of all this time. I was certain I would not come out of there alive. I told the guy shackled to me, "I should've gone with the escape plan while I had the chance." Later I learned some of my friends died trying to escape. They found them floating. They had drowned. The undercurrent at the East River was wicked, and unless you were a good swimmer, the chances of survival were slim. I couldn't swim well but I was willing to take my chances instead of the misery I would be facing in prison. But I thought of my son Anthony. Just about all the guys that went had gotten caught, never making it out of the water, and the ones that did make it off the island were later caught, and now facing new charges.

My spirit was being ripped to pieces as I was dying within. This dark lonesome feeling overcame me and I didn't think I would survive it. My pain turned to suffering. I was going to be locked in a cell for what felt like an eternity and missing out on everything in my son's life. I grew anxious, claustrophobic and felt like I was suffocating. As we got closer to the prison, I checked to see if there was a way to escape, but imagining that fantasy was a waste of time. We pulled up to the eerie looking prison. The walls were so long and tall. There were guards in guard shacks with rifles. I became nauseous as the hair on the back of my neck stood up, and I had goosebumps throughout my entire body. We were welcomed by big 300-pound rednecks yelling and scaring most of us. We entered the reception area and were forced to take showers, shave our heads and all facial hair. We were told the rules, given a rule book and told to learn it like the back of our hand. Then, we were given green prison uniforms with a prison ID number on them. Till today, I still haven't forgot "77B-1399." It's like it's been branded in my fuckin brain. The COs were no joke; they didn't want to hear a peep from us. I had to get used to it because I was going to be there for a very long time—if I ended up living through it all. I needed to get out of this poor me syndrome. I had to get my act together before I lost my fuckin mind.

At the mess hall, there were a few guys I knew. As they were eating, I yelled out one of their names and immediately got into trouble. I got pulled off the line, taken to my cell, and didn't get a chance to eat. I had to learn the hard way, I guess. A lot of people saw me though, and the word spread that I was there. I got an infraction and had to go before a committee to determine my punishment. They gave me an ear full and a warning. It wasn't how I wanted to start my stay. For the next three days, I was in lockup. Whenever I saw anyone I knew after that, we would just nod our heads in recognition. It wasn't until I was transferred into population three months later that I saw Joey again during recreation. It was good to be back with him. We were both so happy. We looked forward every day to recreation so that we could hang out. He found a way to get transferred to where I was. We played chess almost every night from cell to cell calling out pieces.

One day while walking to program through honor block, I ran into my cousin Mambo. I knew he was upstate but didn't know where. We did all we could to find a way to see one another. I was well connected now. We became "The Fosse Posse." We all had jobs in different areas, so we knew plenty of people. From eggs, meat, shanks, or messages to other parts of the jail we were able to get. We had stashes throughout the prison in the event something broke out—it was just the way of prison life.

Early on in prison upstate.

Even though I had gotten some clout in prison, I didn't want to get too comfortable in there. My thinking began to change. I knew that I was growing into my manhood. I was experiencing hope that one day I would be out of here and would see my son again. I was afraid of getting into trouble and spending more time here than necessary, and I began to see how easy it was to fuck up. There were so many losers here with nothing to do but hang and talk shit. The inmates looked for any action to go down as a form of recreation and distraction from the pain and loneliness of doing time. I didn't want to be a part of that any longer. Most times I'd stay locked in my cell reading a book when I knew some shit was going to hit the fan. I did all I could to keep my nose clean. I continued being motivated by the books I read. I was just so excited, that I would even read to other inmates who didn't know how to read. I wanted to change my life around and I felt I could do that through at least freeing my mind. I entered school for my GED, and I took various trainings in electrical, printing and accounting. I was hungry to learn. I was going to take full advantage so that I could re-enter society as a reformed man. This time I wanted to do the right thing.

Although the correction officers controlled the prison, there were gangs all over, from the Latin Kings, Neta, Bloods, and Crips, to the Five Percenters and others. When something went down, they would all come out; and there was always some shit happening. I was cool with all of them. Some groups did not consider themselves to be a gang, but to me, they all seemed the same.

During programming one day, I was called for a visit. I was surprised to see my son with his mother sitting there. This was the first time I had seen him since I got locked up. He had grown so much. I felt emotional and thought I might cry, but I held back just so he wouldn't see my tears. Although much time had passed, he seemed not to have forgotten me. I was so happy to see his cute face again. I held him in my arms and kissed him all over him. She looked really good too. I wanted to hold her in my arms and kiss her as well, but I tried to remain cool because it felt a little uncomfortable. We talked about my son and took some pictures. Towards the end, she told me that she'd be willing to wait for me, but only with the condition that we get married.

As much as I wanted to have someone to ride this out with me, I responded, "If you wait for me and remain faithful, then I will marry you when I get out." She quickly said, "If you don't marry me now, Pepe, you can forget about me forever." I stayed loyal to what I said and didn't budge, and she got up, took my son, and stormed out of there. That was the last time I saw her.

Being separated from my son Anthony was killing me. It would be a long time before I saw him again. One day I begged my brother Ed to find him and bring him to Elmira if she allowed it so I could see him. I did all I could so that he would not forget me. As the years passed, I didn't see him as much anymore. It was just too hard on everyone to take this long trip besides, I didn't want to be a burden on anybody, plus I was running out of options. The only thing I could do was write letters, send pictures and cards for even the silliest of occasions. I never knew if they were getting to him as they kept moving. I just wanted him never to forget me. I held onto those moments I got to spend with him as a baby, how I would hold him in my arms, throw him in the air as he would laugh, and play with his feet as he sat in his crib. He never knew of all the days I cried and longed to hold him in my arms, or how much I truly loved him, and would give my life for him. I missed him so much.

I was really making a lot of progress and was proud of myself. I began to grow acceptance with everything. I felt at ease and a peace came over me. The change was becoming obvious—that is until I called home one day and talked with my sister Cindy. She told me that my son's mother had eloped with her husband Renzo, my best friend growing up. I loved this guy and I could not believe what I was hearing. I listened to my sister cry. She didn't want to tell me this, but I compelled her to. I went into a rage and slammed down the receiver. My heart was torn to pieces. I hurt for both my sister and me. Hate and revenge played through my mind for a very long time. I knew this guy since I was about six or seven years old. Ever since then we'd been in each other's lives. I trusted and loved him with all my heart. How could they have done this to us? I felt betrayed by both of them. My heart bled with endless pain. I felt sad for the kids, especially his daughter-my niece and my son, who I'm sure were confused about whether to call one another cousins or brother and sister. I planned to murder them both when I got out.

It was becoming difficult to concentrate so I played a lot of handball and paddle ball to help distract me from totally losing my mind. The anger was chiseled on my face, where everyone took notice and prisoners would give me space. One knew when not to kid around.

A few years passed and I was doing okay. For my son's sake, I finally surrendered wanting to kill them both. It took me a very long time before I could let that go. I almost lost my mind, and my life, doing dumb shit in prison because of my anger. I became more daring, but I suffered a great deal behind it. I was now releasing it, freeing myself.

I had been in Elmira State Penitentiary for almost one year and with the 18 months in Rikers Island that was 30 months I had been down. In two days, I'd be coming up for a parole board hearing. I was now twenty years old. Although I knew they weren't going to release me, they still had to let me go before the board because of the type of sentence. It was called a "zip bid," what they gave to minors for their first conviction. I expected to get hit with at least 18 months, but I was still preparing myself for their questions. As the day got closer, I grew anxious, and when the day came I was nervous as hell. Joey's case was going before the board as well. It comforted me that he was there. I walked in before him, and from my meeting, I knew it wasn't good. When I got out he asked me how it went and I shook my head. I was escorted back to my cell. I had to wait and see when the mail arrived at night. The mail came and when the guard put it on the bars, it sounded heavy, as if there was more than just paper in the envelope. After a pause, I reached for it and I opened the one sheet of paper inside, and it read, "You are hereby denied parole and your next board hearing will be in 36 months." A sadness came over me. I became silent and wanted to cry. I went into a rage and began throwing and breaking things.

Joey was above me, he knew it was bad, but waited till he got his mail, then asked me, "How much time you got?"

"Three more years," I said.

"Damn," he said.

"How about you?" I asked.

"I got a release date," he said.

We went silent for a while. We both knew what we were thinking, but kept it to ourselves. He was sad for me but happy for him. I was pissed with me, but happy for him.

We spent time together planning his release. He promised to visit and look out for me. His day came and he was released. I missed the shit out of him, and again felt abandoned. At least my cousin was still there to ease my loneliness, but it wasn't the same. I looked up to Joey like a mentor, and learned many things from him, we were tight. Besides, my cousin was somewhere in honor block and Joey was always nearby.

One day during recreation I got a message to "watch my back" again. I knew the issue with the Dominican was going to follow me everywhere. I told a few of my boys, so we were always on guard. Walking through the corridor on my way to programming, I got jumped by a few guys. Some of the cats that knew me came to my defense. The COs came and broke everything up. Soon after, I got the message which said, "You fucked with the wrong guy and you are going to die." I told my cousin Mambo, who'd be responsible if anything were to happen to me.

My cousin was no joke. He had a reputation of his own. He had been down for a while on a murder rap. Everyone had much respect for him in and out of the joint. On the outside, he ran with some big heroin connections and became a cleanup man (hitman). He offered his services to the highest bidder. So, with us both being well connected inside, I wasn't too worried. It would have been hard for those guys to try something. Besides, the guy wasn't at this prison. I needed to learn who this Dominican guy was, how he was connected and to whom, in the event I ever needed such information.

I played the wall everywhere I went. It became the norm. I was never sure if one of this guy's people would try something, so it was easier for me to see everything going on and no one could sneak up from behind me. Those that wanted to talk to me came over to where I was at. I mean you could still get to me if you wanted. I worked out at the weight room, played basketball and hung out at the handball court. I sat with the blacks, broke bread with the Italians, hung out with the Colombians, was cool with the Mexicans, and even most of the Dominicans because I grew up with them in the Heights. Everyone knew I defended the weak. They needed someone to show them the ropes before they became someone's bitch. It's a game inmates play. First they start courting you, making time with you, like we've done on the outside with the broads. They give you smokes, food and candy, and now you owe them. By then, the only way out is to be their girl or, man-up and fight. I remembered how helpless I was when I first got here and no one came to my rescue so I took it upon myself to look out for those helpless scared kids that everyone wanted to use for their personal pleasures or recreation. It was difficult enough for them without having someone fuck with their heads. So if you came to where I housed and you were a booty bandit—you had me to deal with. Most stand up guys respected me for that.

One day, one of my Dominican friends told me that someone from another crew had put a contract out on me and it was paying well. From that moment, it became hard to concentrate. I was always looking over my shoulder. My spirit was troubled, and I became uneasy. I didn't want to come out of my cell for recreation anymore, but sometimes I had to in order not to show fear. I had to put on that mask again. I wasn't sure who took the contract. It could be anybody. For days, it was all I could focus on. I was losing my fuckin mind.

There was this little crowd of guys that I once had some beef with, so I thought it might be coming from there. While in the yard, I strapped down with the shank I had buried in the yard, told my people and then I stepped to them. One of them reacted. A fight broke out, I pulled the shank and I stabbed one of them. I felt a burning. Someone had cut me with something across my stomach and I was bleeding. The COs came running as I passed the shank off and walked away. I put pressure on the wound to slow the bleeding so the COs wouldn't notice. Everyone got sent back to their cells. Afraid to go to sick hall and get caught, I treated the wound myself. I was never certain of where the threat was coming from, but I felt I had to make a statement.

Things slowed down somewhat, but I was still worried. I needed to get out of this place before someone shanked me, or I caught a case. I asked to see my counselor, told him I was having problems there, and asked for a transfer. A month later, I was on a transfer. I was moved around from Clinton, Green Heaven to Comstock and ended up at Woodbourne Correctional, a medium security facility.

It was during the end of the baseball season for the Italians and they were in desperate need of a 3rd baseman. Mario and I knew each other from our travels in the joint, and he heard I was there. He paid me a visit, and asked if I wanted to play on their softball team and I agreed. This helped me get my mind off the unsettling feeling I was having from all the transfers and moving around, which had me unsure if I would even stay there. I was the only Latino on the team, and that year we won the title. In the jailhouse paper, I was named, "Pepe Stone, the human vacuum cleaner at 3rd base."

Hadn't been but a month since I'd been at this new facility when I got a visit from my brother Mike. I was surprised to see both my parents sitting there. My mother looked happy to see me, and my father came sharp with his suit, but he looked sad. He got up to hug me as I kissed him in the cheek. We sat down, and as soon as I asked him how he was doing, he began to cry. He only been there a hot minute and excused himself then left. Mom said he'd been sad knowing his son was in jail and really couldn't deal with it too well. He never came back in and shortly thereafter the visit came to an end. I'd never seen my Pops cry before and that touched me. I understood how he felt.

My Pops.

I continued school, got my GED, and registered into a college program by Sullivan County Community College. I was given outside clearance and worked on the Horticulture program. Although it was still part of the prison, it was outside of the main building without the bars and the daily crap which occurred all day long. Although I couldn't see the outside world, I felt freer; It was a big relief. We were up on a hill surrounded by trees. We were able to cook the vegetables we grew for the prison or, whatever we could get our hands on. The thought of escaping crossed my mind, but I quickly dismissed it when I realized how close I was to my next parole hearing. I could hold on for another two years till then, but if they hit me again, I might just break out. I was doing well and had good grades. Not bad for a guy who didn't like school and couldn't read well. At least I found a little peace of mind, and by now my whole thinking had changed. I was preparing myself for the next appearance at the parole board.

Through my sister Dee I got a message to my past girl Terry and asked if I could write her. We began communicating. She was consistent,

Me and my mom at my graduation.

and every week I looked forward to her letters. She would send me packages and soon began visiting me. She was a special kind of girl. One day she even surprised me and brought Mom up to see me. Mom loved her. For the following visit, I asked her to bring some weed, and she did. Now I was living large in jail, buying the necessities with it, and smoking lovely. We played it cool at the visiting room, mostly holding hands and would sneak a kiss here and there, because I had her sign up as my sister when visiting me so that one day I could get a conjugal visit—It was the shit we did in jail to get over. They only gave those to model prisoners with no infractions, if they were married or to family members. Six months later I got approved, and when the day came, I was so excited. After so many years of not being with a woman, feeling her touch on my body, lying naked, rubbing feet were blissful. Although we dated before, we never had sex. She was an old-fashioned girl, sweet and loving. One of the few girls I respected. She was so in love with me. I let her go back then because I was attracted to the nasty girls. It was all about sex, and because she wasn't letting loose, I hurt her. I remember how everyday she would walk two miles from where she lived to come see me. None of the guys hit on her; not only because she was my girl, but she demanded respect, whether I was there or not, she carried herself like a lady and would have made any man proud, but me... I couldn't see that then.

Now here she was back in my life riding this out with me. We were at the trailer house together for the first time. The anticipation was so high and we were both so nervous. We hugged and kissed, then sat down for a while and talked. It was the first time I had a deep conversation with a woman when the whole intention wasn't just about sex. We talked about the experience of our past and how we were joined together again after so many years. We were just thirteen then, now here we were as adults. We laid down on the couch. She placed her head on my chest as I ran my fingers through her hair. I told her about my experiences, and all my mistakes. She became emotional, and began to cry because of my pain. It was time. We got up and went to the bed. I took her with gentle hands, caressing every corner of her body as we made love. To my surprise, she was still a virgin. We made the best of our thirty hours together as we laid in bed stroking and holding each other tight. When the time came, it was hard to let go.

She kept visiting, and on our next six months, we got approved for another conjugal visit. This time I asked her to bring me a half ounce of weed. I was at the trailer already, waiting and wondering what was taking so long. Looking out the window watching all the wives and family members coming, then it got to where there was no movement, and I started to get anxious. I thought, "Did she let me down at the last minute? Or did she have a problem?"

When I saw the COs walking towards the trailer, I knew the answer. Then came that knock which sunk my heart to the pit of my stomach. I reluctantly opened the door, reached out my hands and the handcuffs were placed on me. She had been busted and was being detained for investigation, and I was on my way straight to Solitary Confinement.

No Regrets

My heart was broken. What did I do? She must have been so scared. I could only imagine what she was going through. Maybe the guards became suspicious about her truly being my sister and decided to look closer. Fortunately, they let her go, but she was no longer allowed to visit. It was the last time I saw her. That shit was killing me. I was messed up. Because of my greed and selfishness, I hurt her. I was mourning the loss of not being able to see her again. I was an emotional wreck. I was back to regretting my mistakes, playing it over and over in my head beating my own ass. I lost the one good thing in my life that mattered. I was surprised they didn't charge either of us with a crime, but I was sure to pay the price at my next parole hearing.

While in solitary confinement, the CO came to my cell to tell me that my family called the facility with the news that my father was dying. The news was hard on me—"My father can't die, why has no one told me that he is sick?" I had the choice of either a pre-death hospital visit or funeral home visit after his death. I chose to see him while he was still alive. Full of emotion, I laid in bed staring at the ceiling reminiscing on everything he and I had been through. The next day I got suited up and was driven to the hospital in New York City. It was a long drive. I prayed my father would live long enough for me to see him to say my goodbyes. We arrived at Columbia Presbyterian Hospital, down the block from where I grew up and where my sons were born. My family was already there. They saw the shackles and weren't sure whether to come close to me or not, but as I kept walking towards them, the guards understood. They all huddled around to hug me. It felt good to see them after such a long time. I was given some private time with them and that's when the shackles were removed. I got much needed love. They were uncertain about how I felt knowing the history between my dad and me. The doctor came in to talk to us. He told us there was nothing more they could do because his liver had burst and now it could be a matter of days. The reality that my father was going to die made me sad. I didn't want to be around all the crying; I wanted to go see him right now—alone. The guards escorted me right to the entrance and let me go in. It was a large ward with patients along each side of the wall and down the middle. His bed was at the far side of the left wall. I walked slowly trying to control my emotions, and preoccupied with how he would receive me if he were awake.

I remember stopping mid-way when I clearly saw him, as if I was not sure what to do. I thought, "Maybe this wasn't a good idea after all." I continued walking very slow in a state of emotional confusion. I got to the bedside. He was resting peacefully in a coma.

As I stood over him, I began thinking about the few times he was good to me. He was a tall 220-pound strong man, and now he laid here looking frail and ready to die, and I was not ready to see him go. So much to say, so much to do, too young to die. It was the very first time I saw him look so vulnerable. I reached out my hand and placed it on his cheek, when suddenly he opened his eyes to look at me.

A tear rolled down his face, and he said in Spanish, "Te estaba esperando para pedir te perdon." (I was waiting for you to ask you for your forgiveness before I die.)

I began to cry uncontrollably, and told him, "I've always loved you Papi, you just never allowed me to show you, but I forgive you and I hope you can forgive me for the pain I caused you."

He nodded his head and closed his eyes. I said my last goodbye and cried all the way back to my family who were there waiting to hug me one more time before I went on my way back to prison.

Throughout the entire ride back I sat quietly with my thoughts. I was sad, and missing my dad already. I was glad to have that opportunity to see him one last time and forgive him, but now I would never see him again. At that moment, I truly felt his love come over me, and I erased everything he ever did to me. I just wished he could hold me in his arms and love me just once. I wanted him to stroke his little boy reassuring him everything was now going to be alright. I was gonna miss him.

I returned to the jail and was escorted back to solitary confinement to complete the remaining time of my punishment. Late that night, I got the news, my father had died. I hit the floor and sobbed like a baby.

The stay in solitary was hard, but I finally made it out. I was ready to get back to normalcy. The guys were glad I was back, but as soon as I saw certain individuals, all the joy of being back in population went away. I still couldn't shake the issue with this guy from my mind. I needed to keep my guard up. It was like a heavy weight I carried on my shoulder everywhere—at the gym, playing ball, watching TV, cooking, studying. It tired me mentally. I continued being vigilant and playing the wall so no one could come behind me. But if they wanted war, I was ready to bring it.

Six months after finishing the college program with thirty-two credits, I was scheduled to go before the parole board for the second time. The night before I was filled with anxiety and could not sleep. I was sure—almost sure, I would be denied again as they found my crime to be too heinous. Either way, although I longed for freedom, this time it really didn't matter. There was not much more they could do to me. I was not far from already serving two-thirds of my time, and by law they couldn't hold me, unless of course, I caught a new charge.

Regardless of what I told myself, I was still nervous. I cleaned up nicely to make an impression. I took a seat next to the other 25-30 guys waiting to be called. I tried to be cool by showing no fear while looking at all the other blank faces, but as I sat there waiting to be called, my hair was already droopy from all the sweating I did. Everyone was silent; all you could hear was the sounds of beating hearts and built-up hopes. I was tensed and my knees could not stop shaking. I saw the guys before me come out of the board's office with sad faces and I said to myself in silence "Shit, I am doomed." Finally my name was called and my knees almost locked on me as I began walking. I was told to take a seat, as they began reading my charges and my jailhouse record. I sat there trying to be relaxed and not worry about the outcome. Here I was once again being judged by three people that held the key to my freedom.

They asked me, "Why should we let you go?"

I answered, "I know I committed a horrible crime. I was a senseless teen with no direction. I came here as a boy, and now I am a man. I learned some things about myself since I got locked up. The pain of being incarcerated was a rude awakening, and I have accomplished many things to help me change my life to become a productive member of society. However, if you feel deemed to continue my punishment, I understand and will not be bitter. I will finish out my time because there is nothing more one could do to me that hasn't already been done."

I got dismissed. The guys waiting their turn looked at me—as we had done with everyone else that came out, and I pretended to be tough, when in fact I was almost shitting in my pants. I was escorted back to my cell where I eagerly awaited the mail that evening. The CO placed an envelope on the bars. I sat there for about 15 minutes staring at it; then I got up and grabbed it. I sat back on my bed holding it with both hands afraid of seeing the rejection, yet hoping for my freedom. I asked God for his will and confided that I would accept the outcome if he felt I wasn't ready. I opened the letter slowly. It read, "You have been granted release." I became very emotional and fell to my knees. I cried, thanking God. Finally, after six long years I was going to be a free man.

CHAPTER 6

My Sons

waited anxiously for my release date. The two-month wait suddenly felt far away. I was making plans for everything I needed and wanted to do. No longer did I want to come out of my cell at rec time for fear of something happening to make me lose my release date. Nor did I try sharing my release date with anyone because there were plenty of lifers that really didn't need to hear about it. And with all the jealous individuals, it was too easy getting trapped into doing something. Even here there were a lot of haters. I felt more and more anticipation as the date got closer. It just wasn't coming fast enough, and I needed to occupy my mind. Somehow, I was unable to focus or think about anything else.

The date finally came. It was early summer 1981 and I was going home. I felt alive and happy. I tried hard to contain my excitement, as the guys were wishing me well saying our last goodbyes. Suddenly from nowhere, I heard a voice yell, "That contract still follows you." Normally I would let the thought of that kind of threat consume me, but the only thing on my mind was getting out of this joint and going to find my son. I wasn't going to let some lame ass bitch mess up the day I'd been waiting for; there would be plenty of time to think about that later. The big iron gates opened. I felt like running through them, but I contained my excitement. As they closed behind me, I stood there for a few minutes, took a deep long breath into my lungs—awh, this is what freedom smells like. I got on my knees, kissed the ground and thanked God. I got up, took the polyester jacket to my state suit, threw it in the air, then headed to the train station. I sat in silence, in complete awe, looking out the window absorbing everything I saw and missed. Everything appeared so fresh and colorful, and the grin on my face spoke many words.

I arrived at the New York City Port Authority bus terminal with $40 in my pocket. I imagined one day being back and here I was. I walked up and down 42nd Street for hours reminiscing about old times in the early 70's. Back then there was nothing but peep shows, sex movie theaters, prostitution, homosexuality and lots of drugs. It was an active place. All the

75

A picture of me in prison.

school haters would cut class, and head downtown to catch the matinee. It was the time when pimps were a big thing, and movies like Super Fly, and The Mack were the hot ticket. I was always fascinated watching how the pimps operated and the money they made. I saw how the girls moved around, got into cars, and ran when they saw the cops. It seemed like a hard ass job, yet there were so many of them; and the pimps, with their fur hats and fine clothes watching all the action from a block away. They were shooting the breeze with each other, strutting their style—this shit was so cool.

One day I thought, "I'm gonna be a pimp." I had all the swag, charisma, looks and style to be one, but convincing some girls to do this was another story. I cared too much about women to have them live this sorry-ass life, it was like slavery. The women must be crazy to give all their money to some smooth-talking dude and repeat the game day after day. It is no wonder, that many of them turned to drugs to numb themselves, to be able to deal with the life they were now stuck in. I identified with this.

At the same time, there was also this big gay movement going on. I remember this guy called "Lollipop." He was the most popular in the

No Regrets

"Deuce"—street slang for 42nd Street—and of course gay. Along with some other gay guys, he controlled the drug game; everyone was always around him. I was too young to be hanging with them, but he allowed me to because I had no place to go. He looked at me like a son, and protected me from the other gay vultures. At that time, Quaaludes were the "in" thing. I liked Lollipop; he never put a hand on me and made it clear to everyone to respect me. He was good to me, he gave me money to eat, kept an eye on me, and only gave me drugs once in a while because I begged him to, but he watched me closely. It was during a time when I was lost and looking to belong. I never really felt a part of anything and in my search for identity, they represented a sense of "free spirit and happiness" and I really enjoyed hanging with them. When the weather would break, we'd all head down to the fountain at Central Park, where we would meet up with a bunch of his friends. You talk about fun—that was some wild stuff. These cats knew how to party. After doing a Quaalude, come nightfall, we would sleep right there on the grass and start all over again at day break. Even when Lollipop wasn't around, I remember spending many days and nights there in that part of Central Park. It was a carefree time.

There was nothing in the world more interesting than being at the "Deuce." Now everything appeared so clean and different, but the memories lasted a lifetime. Everything was now in the past: the scars, the Deuce, Andrea, Renzo, prison, and all that pain I suffered. I was a kid yesterday and my whole life had been about yesterday. Now, here I was a grown man, reflecting on the past, but it was about today and a whole lot of tomorrows.

I came back to reality, and thought about where I was going to lay my head. After reporting to the parole office, I went to my sister Dee's house in the Bronx. She welcomed me inside and fed me. Afterward, I went on a mission to find my son Anthony. I prayed that when and if I found him he would receive me well and know how much I missed him. I was excited and couldn't wait to see him.

I discovered where my son and his mother lived. Respectfully, I went by there and I called out the window. My son's mother came to the window; her face paled as if she saw a ghost. I noticed she got emotional then quickly put her head back inside. I waited with open arms for my son to come outside. He gingerly approached me. I held him for what seemed like an eternity. He stood there awkwardly with his arm gently around my neck as if he was uncertain what to do. I understood. I didn't know what to do or say other than I missed and loved him very much. When I left him he was just a year old, now seven, he seemed like a big boy. So much catching up to do. But right then, I just wanted to take in the moment.

After spending some time with him, I promised to be back. Every weekend I had the same routine, I went to my son's window and yelled out his name. When he saw me, he came down and met me. One day my son's mother came to the window, and she stayed there staring at me. She and Renzo had since married, and in the six years I was gone they had two children of their own. She stayed there long enough with our eyes locked on each other, when suddenly Renzo came to the window, snatched her in and asked me, "What do you want with my wife?" Just the sound of that didn't seem right and I began to feel a rush come up within me. It took me a second before it registered in my brain. I began to feel the pain all over again, along with some jealousy. It was the first time I had seen him since the time he came to visit me at Rikers Island after he got released. That was when he promised me he would look out for my girl and son. He sure did a good job of that.

"You dirty piece of trash. Why don't you come down and meet me man to man?" I shouted out to him.

He closed the window. I waited outside for him, but he never came down. My son didn't come down either. From that point, I was informed through a family member that if I wanted to see my son, I had to have someone call to say I was coming. I would then have to wait down the block for my son. I knew if I wanted to see him, I had to comply.

I tried to remain in my son's life to the best of my ability. I did what I could without trying to start trouble or make it harder for me to see him. He was growing up fast. I would pick him up on the weekends, and we would have fun. I made every attempt to see him even if only to see his face and him mine. As he got a little older, we began hanging out. He would stay with me, and we'd go everywhere. Any girl I was with during that time would just have to deal with it because my son came first. He was a good kid, and I liked when he was with me. We were making up for lost time.

I didn't know how to be a dad, but we had good times when I would pick him up. He loved riding in my car. Then we would go find an open fire hydrant, and wash the car while blasting the hip hop and rap music he liked. During the summertime, open fire hydrants were pretty much everywhere. This was how city kids kept cool in those hot summer months. This became our pastime. We bonded and had a lot of fun doing so. It felt so good to watch his excitement about being with me. We were off to a great start, and I looked forward to being together. Our main event was when the car show would come to the Jacob Javits Convention Center in downtown Manhattan. We couldn't wait—he loved that. What I didn't know how to do was show emotions or express my love, which I think he needed most.

Years passed and he was now about seventeen. Our relationship was great. The biggest mistake I ever did was to try and be hip in his eyes. One day I offered him a drink, and some years later we began smoking weed together. Then one day I treated him to hookers, and then came the cocaine. Although he thought I was the coolest dad ever, something began to change. I believe that was the moment I lost his respect as a father. No matter what I did, it would never change. The things we did were not what a father should do with his child. He learned about image and ego from me. He'd watch me rapping to all the girls and thought I was hip—that's not what I wanted for him. I always felt I needed to entertain him. As uncomfortable as it was, I only did what I knew. It was all about presents, money, and cars. That was how I knew to please him, and I wanted him to be happy when he was with me. I could see his boredom and dissatisfaction when there was nothing to do but watch TV. I know it must've been hard on him not having me around, and having another man raise him. He expressed little to no emotion, and I could see he was growing hard.

Over time, we grew closer and became very much a part of each other's life. One day he got in a terrible motorcycle accident that banged him up pretty bad. After a few weeks, he was discharged but still on pain meds. Between the pain and the medication, I could tell he wasn't all there. We got into a discussion about the medication that turned into an argument and he became defensive. Maybe it was my approach. I do know I'm a little rough around the edges. He physically threatened to hurt me and then threw me out of the house. This is when I felt he had totally lost respect for me.

I could feel the love and respect a child has for a father was vanishing. As much as it hurt, I knew something inside both of us had changed. I felt his pain and his anger. The bitterness and hatred he harbored for me finally surfaced, and some hurtful, mean words were exchanged. My heart got ripped from my chest. I felt this sorrow for him, but at the same time I was angry. I wasn't sure if this was all because of my past, his mother's fault, or the damage his stepfather Renzo did to him. He once told me about the years of abuse he and his mom endured and how much he hated Renzo, who had since walked out on her and the kids when Anthony was in his mid-teens. They got divorced, and in 2016, Renzo had a motorcycle accident and died.

Now, here I was with him face to face, listening to him insult me. I was becoming angrier, and the ugly guy I had long buried began to surface. As the noise in my head grew louder, we both lost it. I stood there numb, and for a brief second, I caught this flash of my father's face which fright-ened me, and it interrupted me from going further and I left. Up the block, I sat in my car for an hour while I cried and let the anger pass. I'm not sure if my father was telling me something, or if it was just divine intervention, but whatever it was, I am grateful. I was never aware of the intensity of An-thony's feelings for me, but I'm glad he freed himself, even if, sadly, it was at the expense of our relationship. I wanted so badly to believe that he loved me. I thought maybe it was his current state of mind which caused him to flip out on me, but the pain was too deep and the damage was done—we lost each other forever. He and I are so much alike on so many levels. We are head strong, self-centered, and most times we don't see anyone's point but our own. He once made an attempt to apologize via text, and the follow-ing two days or so, he came over to my house because he needed a favor. I thought it was an excuse for him to come by so we could sit down and clear the air about what happened—maybe cry a little and forgive each other. At this point it didn't matter what reason he used, I was just happy to know we'd have this opportunity to talk and I would have my boy back in my life. But that was not his plan. He came for what he needed, made a promise to get back with me, and then left. I stood there stunned with my jaw dropped as he walked out. In the past, it didn't affect me as much that he used me—although I'd bitch a little, I would let him get away with it just to please him; however, this time it was different. I saw what little regard he had for our relationship or my feelings. That was the last time I heard from him.

No Regrets

It's been a year since that incident and we still haven't connected. The wedge between us as father and son grew, but I still love and miss him very much. My hope is that one day we can find forgiveness for one another.

Over the years, his mother and I established communication. As adults, we were able to make amends to one another. Although our relationship throughout the years had been volatile, we had come a long way from that fourteen-year-old kid she met. I'm sure she still hurts because she always kept the hope that one day we'd get back together. Even after all the forgiveness, our relationship can still be rocky, so we keep it at a distance now.

I had no skills on how to be a dad. My parenting skills with my second-born son Alex were no better. I met his mom Bella at a drug detox. We ended up having sex in one of the back rooms near the storage closet, and he was conceived. Before leaving rehab, she gave me the keys to her house and told me I could stay there. A few days later she got out and we lived together. I was trying hard to stay clean, but after about a week of getting out, she began using again, and it wasn't long before I too picked up the habit. Thereafter, the drama began. I kept finding things missing and money gone. There was no trust, only arguments. It was an insane relationship for the four months or so it lasted, until I got busted again on a gun rap. She came to see me at Rikers Island and that's when I first saw her belly— I never knew she was pregnant. She suggested we get married while I was awaiting the outcome of the case. I told her no, but if she stayed faithful, when I got out, we could discuss it. She did the same as my first son Anthony's mother—she never came back and got with someone else. She gave birth while I was in jail. Two years later I got released. After I knew where I was going to lay my head and put my bags down, I went out looking to find and meet my new son Alex for the first time.

I got to the building where I once lived with her. I walked up the stairs and I knocked on the door. I saw the look of surprise when she opened the door. She introduced me to my son and we had a good visit together. He was a handsome boy. I continued visiting him once a week and giving her what little money I could. He was a momma's boy and appeared to be very spoiled. Whatever he cried for he got. He was a baby brat. Many times I wanted to tell her she was raising my son as a wimp, but was afraid of her response. In his early years of public school, his mom would call me just about every week because he was always getting into trouble and disrespecting his teacher.

With Alex this became very challenging for me and I didn't know how to discipline him, or even talk with him because he would just lose control. He'd become very aggressive towards his mom, and anyone that told him anything he didn't want to hear. I saw the anger and I knew this was not going to be easy. Tactically, I strategized my approach, but most times it was useless; he would just rebel saying, "no one understands me," and cried that it was everyone else's fault and not his. He fought everyday not to go to school. His mother drove me crazy with him, but I also had no control over him. No matter what I said, he just sat there with a face hoping I would shut up and leave already. Not long after that he stopped going to school all together. All he wanted to do was hang on the block, so the streets did what they do—they sucked him up, and I watched as his life became a mess. I saw me in him, and I knew he was going to have a hard core existence. His attitude about everything and everyone only got worse and no one could say a thing to him. He was now living a "thug life."

Now twenty-nine years old, he is still the same, going down the same path as I did. We have no relationship or communication. I feel it wouldn't matter to him if I died tomorrow. I don't think he really ever accepted me as his father. He loved his stepfather very much. Once he even told me that this guy was his real dad. Although at the time it hurt, I wasn't mad, I understood. However, it never stopped me from looking for him or trying to make a difference in his life. He now has three children of his own from two different women. I was hoping he'd become a better father to them than I ever was to him, but that doesn't seem to be the case.

I learned that Alex had gotten arrested and sent to Rikers Island. As much as I dreaded going back there, I had to visit my son. I felt it was my obligation to school him with my knowledge from my stay there so he could be better equipped than I was. The reality of being back there was overwhelming, but I had to contain my emotions.

It broke me to pieces looking at my own son sitting there in a jailhouse jumpsuit. "I'm not going to cry," I told myself, as I continued walking towards him. I hugged him tightly and told him, "I love you." What I wanted to do, was get the hell out of there as fast as I could; I was feeling uncomfortable.

We exchanged words and I told him, "This will be the one and only time I will come to see you here." We hugged and we kissed goodbye, and I left there feeling sad for him, but from here on in, he would have to learn from his own experiences, and the choices he made he would have to own.

In 2009, Alex's mom passed away. I know he felt alone. He had no relationship with his other two siblings who lived elsewhere. His life spun out of control even more, and I couldn't do anything to save him from himself.

My kids never really knew my struggles growing up, the times when I was homeless going from shelter to shelter, having the little I had be stolen, and feeling like I was back in prison all over. Many nights I couldn't even sleep thinking some nut job would stab me. They were times I rode the A train up and down till morning trying to rest and get my thoughts in order. Other times, I was staying at the Boys Club in Harlem, or with some other woman, until I got my own place through Section 8. I was ashamed and humiliated going to the welfare department waiting in line to get food stamps, trying to cover my face so no one would recognize me. I had to swallow my pride to survive. It was those struggles along with everything else, that made me thrive. I made my bones, and became who I am. It wasn't easy on my kids, nor was I going to be an enabler to them. It was important to show them tough love, as hard as that was to do. Maybe one day they'll understand that. I know I fell short, but I hoped that they'd be better fathers than I was. Walking around with a grudge and blaming everyone for their situation was not resolving a thing. Of course, not being of sound mind myself, things just got worse. However, there comes a point where we need to man up, take responsibility for the role we played, and stop misdirecting all that hurt bottled up within. I often think about them, and it saddens me. We all had a rough lesson with pain and the past, and it really hurt me to see how they suffered from me not being with them and their mom as a family growing up together. It was important to have been around and teach them how to play catch, and the things dads did when they were young and learning. I could never change this now, and the pain is real—a child needs his dad. I wished it would've been different for us all. I gave what I could, and I'm sure they wanted more than I knew how to give.

I no longer have any excuses. I made some terrible choices in my youth, and it affected the lives of my boys. By the choices we made, we robbed ourselves of the joy of being a family. We were not stuck because we didn't let go, but because we couldn't. The hurt and animosity were too deep. I got lost in my sadness and I couldn't be there for my children the way they expected me to. I'm sure they have their own story to tell; maybe they reacted the only way they knew. I pray that one day they can forgive me as I have forgiven them, and hopefully, be able to sit down as men, reflect on our lives and enjoy each other's company. I hope I live long enough to see this.

As for me, I've tried to rectify where I fell short with them by being a good grandfather to their children, whom I adore and try to spend as much time within their lives as possible. Sadly, one of my grandchildren was lost to the system when the child was only three and was adopted by another family. That was a sad moment when I truly felt powerless and even guilty, wondering if I could've done more to save my first-born grandchild. He should now be about eleven. I still have hope that one day he and I will meet again. Even with all the drama between my sons and me, I never stopped loving them, and will always be available for either one should they ever need my wisdom.

CHAPTER 7

The Game

Making loot and chilling.

My girl Terry was really happy to see me. She forgave me for putting her in the position I did at the prison when she got caught bringing in the weed. She was living with her uncle and his wife in the Bronx. I was able to hang with her there for a little while until I got busy trying to get adjusted to freedom and my new life.

New York City—the energy was electrifying. It was a magical time to be free. Orchard Beach was off the chain. The music, people, and the beautiful women were enticing. I missed out on a lot of things, but now I was enjoying the sights. I ran into some of the Italian guys I met upstate, and they wanted to put me on. I wasn't quite ready for the cocaine game, but I took their numbers and kept it moving to enjoy my first day back at the beach. There is nothing I liked better than walking on Orchard Beach Boardwalk. It's like a bikini fashion show with heels. It was where everyone hung out to meet up with each other or to just watch people as they strolled on by. The guys whistling at the girls, and the girls loving the attention. Every section had their own music and crow. People all around were dancing and having a good time. If you were looking to find someone, at the boardwalk is where you found them. I saw many people I haven't seen in a while—it was a great homecoming.

I got a hook-up with a summer job at the NYC Parks Department. I enjoyed working outdoors, especially when they asked me to work the weekends at the beach—I never turned that down. I got paid while I played. Although he could never find me, the supervisor was always looking for me. He knew I was goofing off, or talking to some girl somewhere. As a punishment, he took away my weekend overtime at the beach and put me to work in one of the parks late afternoons cleaning and monitoring the pool after closing hours. It wasn't long before I started having pool parties, and when he got wind of it, that's when my trouble began and I got fired. I submitted tons of job applications, but after getting fired from the City, no one wanted to hire me.

I had nothing and began to worry. I needed to make money. I remembered my friend Freddie that was upstate with me. Freddie was a smart and very serious older man. He hated the drug business and everyone that dealt with it. We practiced con games, picking locks, safe cracking, learning different schemes and how to commit the perfect crime. I was his student and I was good. The last few years of his sentence, we spent most of the time studying. I was willing to do and learn anything to survive on the outside, no matter what. When Freddie got out, he told me to look him up.

I was curious to see what Freddie was doing so I gave him a call to check in. He didn't want to say much on the phone so he invited me to his home. He owned a beautiful two-story brick house in Pelham Bay that was fully paid off, yet the guy never had a job. His wife made us some lunch as we talked about adjusting to the outside world. He told me to take it easy for a while. He gave me $30k in counterfeit twenties and told me to have fun. And when the money ran out, if I wanted to get busy, to let him know. I started buying little things with the counterfeit bills to get cash back everywhere I went. It was an easy game. I wasn't hurting anyone, and I was getting myself together.

I needed to get away. I decided to take a little trip somewhere, before anything else happened. After being locked up for so long, it was necessary. I needed to figure out what I wanted to do with my future. I took my first trip outside of New York City. I packed my bag and headed to Miami Beach. I wanted to relax and watch the girls in their bikinis.

After a day of enjoying the beach and the sights, I decided to look up an old friend I knew from 163rd Street. He picked me up at my hotel and we went out for a drink. He told me he had seen Joey once at a strip club dancing. I asked him to take me there. We got there, and sure enough, there he was on stage. Joey did a double-take when he saw me and smiled. After his set, he came over with his little "G String," and hugged me. He went back to change, we talked, had a few drinks, and went back to my hotel room to pack my things. I ended up staying with him for the rest of my vacation. I went with him to every gig and met a lot of women, most of them strippers. Miami was the place to be. Joey and I picked up where we left off. It was as if we never missed a beat.

He told me of some work he might have and asked if I wanted in. Just like that, I was back in the game. We planned a few heists and went back to work. We took a trip to Chicago where we set up a club owner and hit a jewelry store. They were selling cocaine out of it, and we struck it big. Then we headed to New York with a quarter million dollars and diamonds. We counted money all night and into the morning while we drank champagne and snorted blow. I noticed Joey was spending a lot of time in the bathroom while he left me counting money. I found that a little off. When he came out his demeanor seemed different. It was well into morning, we were tired, so we ended up stacking money piles together and when they looked alike we each would take one. By his attitude, I knew he just wanted to get me out of his house.

We were living large. Joey got an apartment out in Long Island and I got one in the Bronx. When we wanted to see one another, we would travel in our new Cadillacs. We were living the dream. It was the score I'd been waiting for, the one that was finally gonna put me over the top and solve all my problems. We hit all the clubs and after-hours spots from Long Island to the Bronx, and everywhere in between.

I was becoming a little concerned with Joey's behavior. What I didn't know was that he was harboring some ill feeling towards me. I asked him if something was wrong; then he began telling me that he suspected I pocketed ten grand the night he left me counting money. At that moment I was convinced that he was in the bathroom smoking crack that day. The mistrust was always there from the first time I stashed a ring on him during one of our robberies, along with him thinking I may still be holding onto the situation with my ex and him the day at The Knights club. Just like his brother Mickey, neither one ever trusted or believed in me. Our relationship was in question, and some time later, he moved back to Florida.

It had been some months since I was home. The year was coming to an end and a new year ready to begin. It was my first Christmas and New Years in a long time and I was excited. The holidays were always the hardest being locked up. You could feel the inmate's pain by the look on their face. The whole atmosphere was depressing. One time I wanted to feel Christmas so bad, I stole some paint and drew a Christmas tree on my cell wall. I didn't get to enjoy it because it got me put in solitary confinement throughout the entire holiday for destroying state property. Now I could have my own seven-foot Christmas tree. I was free in the Big Apple, ready to party my ass off. Terry had invited me to spend Christmas with her family. I called Mom up to ask her if she wanted to spend the holiday with me—she was delighted to. I called my son Anthony and he was also happy to spend it together. I took a shower, unwrapped my new suit and shoes that I bought, put on some Aramis cologne and was on my way to pick up my family looking like Tony Montana from Scarface. This was going to be the best day of my life. The party was swinging. Terry was happy to see us. Her family all knew about me and they welcomed me with open arms, all except her dad; he was making me a little uncomfortable. I guess I couldn't blame him—a convict with his baby girl. But I soon dismissed him and went on to dance with Mom then Terry. It was just how I imagined it to be. We had a great time.

Terry and I hung out a lot at my crib, but when things got rough for her at her uncle's, she wanted to move in with me. That's when my feelings began to change. I didn't want to be tied down in a relationship—it's not what I wanted, and it was too soon for that. I felt awful telling her that and offered to help her look for a place She was surprised at my response and I know I hurt her. Despite her disappointment, she said she understood. I mean, I needed to get a lot out of my system before I settled down, and so I did, and shortly thereafter, we broke up.

I began seeing this new girl. She was hot. I could say I was feeling love once again. It was mid-January I believe, when I got a call from a friend I met in prison about doing a job at a Credit Union in Boston, so I went out there to scope the joint out. I contacted Joey in Florida, and he was on the next flight out. After looking at it closer, we thought it was too risky and decided not to go through with it. The Boston crew was disappointed. We asked to be dropped at the bus terminal. On the way there, the pissed driver was speeding despite us telling him to slow down for fear of getting pulled over. His response was "leave the driving to me." Five minutes later the cops were behind us and over the radio told us to pull over. I could've strangled this fuckin dude right there. We got searched and arrested for weapons possession along with the equipment that we brought to pull off the bank job. It hit the Boston Herald front page headline like this: "Three men arrested for attempting to pull off a large heist when their plot was disrupted by police officers."

No Regrets

I wanted to kill the fucker. Joey and I decided, the first opportunity we got, we were going to do a number on him. A few days later at the court-house, everyone got bailed out except me. My parole officer put a warrant out on me so I couldn't make bail. I was beating my own ass with regret. I was stuck in Boston away from everything and everyone. I thought, "How long would my girl be able to deal with this? What am I gonna do now? I am toast."

My world was once again turning upside down. I had forgotten all I learned and what I told myself. Even with all the pain, experience, and knowledge of what not to do, I wasn't able to do the right thing. Logically I understood all that, but thought I was slick. It was the greed, the fear of being broke, my insecurities, and always trying to find an easy way up to success—this was my weakness. I didn't see me making it any other way; I wanted the fast way up and now there was hell to pay.

A week later, coming back from court, the officer told me the warrant was lifted and I could make bail. My girl was staying at a nearby hotel getting ready to leave back home when I called her to come quickly to bail me out. I thought it was some mistake but I wasn't gonna question it. I made the bail and we hauled ass outta there before someone found out. Back home, I called the parole officer to thank him for lifting the warrant, he told me he didn't and that I actually needed to turn myself in immediately.

I said, "This was not a mistake and I made bail, so no, I'm not turn-ing myself in until you find out what happened." I hung up on him and went into hiding to buy some time to make arrangements and get some things in order. Seven days later I called him back and turned myself in, hoping it would work in my favor at the hearing.

Needless to say, nothing worked in my favor. I was slammed with the maximum and was given two more years on a parole violation. I was taken to Ossining Correctional Facility, better known as Sing Sing; where all the notorious gangsters were waiting on death row. It had only been a few months, but it was the hardest prison time I've ever done. I felt hopeless, and was kicking my own ass for being such a fool by risking my freedom knowing very well what I had suffered before. I just couldn't believe what I'd done and now the gates of hell opened up and swallowed me in. The pain was deep. I wondered, "Am I brain-dead or just stupid? Why does the fear of being broke, the greed, have this much power over me?"

I didn't have to go through orientation or all the stuff that the new guys did, because I was a parole violator. I was given some new green with my old number "77B-1399," and sent to B Block population with other violators. Being so close to the City, one was able to get just about anything there. The Italians were living large, eating steak and cooking their own pasta in 7 Block. It was the honor block for the trustees who pretty much were able to move freely around the jail with a pass, moving their stuff, and making money; you had to have juice to be there. But I was doing hard time. My only escape was paddle ball, and every time I slapped that ball, it was like I wanted to kill it. The guys didn't enjoy playing with me, I was too serious, and no matter how hard I slammed the damn ball, I couldn't release the anger. It only got worse.

Joey came to visit me, but thereafter, I never saw him again. After only two visits, my girl stopped coming to see me as well and would not answer my calls. I was broken-hearted one more time. This was the hardest time I had ever done. I was so pissed and angry that I wanted to take it out on others. My whole attitude was raw; I would rather just die than be a failure. The pain was so intense and was killing me slowly.

I saw pictures of my girl wearing the jewelry I had stashed from the robbery with Joey. I had left her money for necessities, living expenses, and to continue paying my rent so when I got out I wouldn't be homeless, but she was partying, eating at nice restaurants, buying new clothes, spending my money, and on top of that, I learned she let my apartment go. The picture I had of her on the cell wall, I used as a punching bag and spat on it. She was going to pay when I got out. I kinda knew she wasn't the girl for me, but I didn't listen to my conscience. I was at the end of my rope in despair and hatred. Every day was a challenge to just stay alive, while my insides were eating me up.

It was June, six months later, while taking out my anger playing paddle ball in the yard, they called me to return to the cell block. The CO told me to pack up I was going home. I thought it was some sick joke being played on me, but it wasn't funny. I told the CO this was a bad joke, but he insisted it was not a joke. I was in disbelief. I went to my cell and began packing, taking my time in case this was a joke, because if it was, someone was going to pay a heavy price. When they took me to retrieve my property, I started to believe that it wasn't a joke, but I still wasn't totally convinced. I walked past the intake reception, going faster and faster. I began sweating and my adrenaline pumped harder; I kept thinking any minute someone would call me back. It wasn't until I was out of the front gate that I knew this was no joke. I beat the case on a technicality, and the Boston case was also dismissed because they found that the arresting officer was corrupt and had been taking payoffs and falsifying arrest records. Not sure what would've happened if another day went by. I couldn't believe it—I was free!

I took the Amtrak train to the city, and here I was back on 42nd street with nowhere to go or stay again. I walked around till I decided to go to my girl's sister's house whom she'd been staying with. The sister was surprised to see me but let me in. We got along well and she was always very nice to me. She told me her sister was not there. I asked her if I could stay there a few nights until I could make some moves and get on my feet. She felt bad for what her sister had done to me and said yes, but didn't want any fighting in the house. About an hour later, I heard the keys at the door. I stood up, hiding at the end of the kitchen until she got in, and then I popped out. She had a shocked expression on her face and wasn't sure what to do. She attempted to go back out, did a retake, and began running into my arms, and kissed me as I stood there motionless with my hands at my side feeling cold.

I said, "Let's take a walk and talk," so we wouldn't argue in the house as I promised. She didn't want to. I grabbed her by the hand and dragged her out.

Exiting the building, I noticed a car double parked with a guy sitting inside. With her head, I saw her signaling him to leave. He looked straight at me and took off. The picture had just come together. She couldn't deny she knew him and I grilled her harder, until she admitted dating him. I grabbed her by her neck, and told her she was going to call him back and tell him I wanted to meet him. I tried keeping my cool so I could learn more, but she was terrified. I learned he was a cop and that he knew all about me. She made the call, and the guy showed up at the house.

I introduced myself, and I asked him to sit. Everyone including my girl's sister was tense. They knew I was heated and they were afraid I would start something. I sensed his fear and used that to my advantage. I started by telling him that I know he knew all about me as I knew about him, but we were here to talk about her.

I said, "I'm going to ask my girl a question, and based on her answer, I will determine the reply." I turned to her and asked, "Do you want him or me?" She paused then replied, "I want you (me)." I looked at the guy and said, "There goes your answer, now, like a man accept it, get up, and get the fuck out, I don't ever want to see your face again."

She sat there in silence and fear as he walked out. "Now, I want you to get me the remaining money and jewelry you have of mine." I demanded.

I looked inside and was really pissed when I saw what little there was. I took the items she had on—rings, earrings and necklace. I packed everything and said I'd be back, and then walked out the door. I thought of never coming back, but that was too easy, she had to pay. I went to see my fence and unloaded it all, then headed back with a plan. We went to bed, and I screwed her with the rough intent of hurting her, as she deserved, and without any emotion. The harder I did it, the more she liked it. Every day, she tried convincing me how much she loved me and how sorry she was, but I wasn't buying it—my mind was set, and every night I did the same thing—acted cold and had rough sex. I felt disconnected from her and I wanted her to feel my pain. She sensed my displeasure, but accepted it—she knew she had wronged me. One day I said, "I'll be back," and I never returned. When she saw me next—she knew it was over—I was holding hands with another girl. As the years went by, I got over the hurt and moved on. We lived in the same area so we often saw each other. No matter what boyfriend she was with, we continued seeing each other and having sex, only this time without the hostility. I guess I still had feelings for her.

It was summer, one of my favorite times of the year. There was a particular smell in the air as everyone got ready for the summer. The girls broke out their tight, short, white pants, and the guys showed off their new sneakers. Everyone joined the gym to get their bodies beach ready. I started dating girls all over the place. It was as if a beast got loose from his cage and had to feed. One night I was at the club alone and at my table, there was a note. I thought it was a number from one of the girls that was checking me out. I opened the paper, and it read, "It isn't over." My heart sank to the floor. I looked up and saw this guy walking away. The cocaine I had been snorting had me paranoid. I looked around, got my things, and immediately got out of there. That night I couldn't sleep. I stayed awake till late morning thinking. Then it hit me! To be free of this threat and stay alive, I had to clean house. I had one friend I knew who could help me do it.

I took a ride into Manhattan looking for Harry. I found him on 167th Street, on the corner of Audubon. The block was active. There was a line almost to the corner of Amsterdam waiting to cop some dope. He was doing good for himself slinging this shit. We stepped away from the crowd and hung out at the restaurant. He offered me a cut in their game; I declined. I wasn't into heroin. I always felt it was a dirty game. He then threw a roll of bills on the table for me. I pushed it back and I told him I was alright. It was customary to do this when you're on top and your boy got out the joint, but that's not why I was there. We ate, laughed and talked about old times. Now was the time to get serious and tell him the real reason why I was here.

I asked him, "Do you remember the pact we made as kids?"

"How could I ever forget?" he said.

"Well my life is in danger and I need help."

He paused, looked at me for a moment and responded, "Who, when, what and where?"

Now, it was on.

CHAPTER 8

Revenge

Harry and me in younger days.

It was the era of cocaine and crack. Washington Heights was the cocaine capital of the world. The Heights had a mixed population of Cubans, Blacks, Whites, Puerto Ricans, Jews and Dominicans. There were BMWs, Mercedes Benzes, and Lexuses everywhere. Music blasted throughout the streets. I thought—"No one works around here?" It was like a party everywhere. Cars with out-of-state license plates would come to buy drugs there. From the outside, it seemed like a different world. People hung out on the corners, drinking, laughing and having fun. Things were moving fast. Everyone was hustling or selling something. Fifteen to twenty guys would rush anyone or their car, trying to make a sale. They would then take you upstairs to a barren apartment with only a desk, a chair and a scale on top of it. There were always three or four guys; one would open the door, another walked you in, another watched everything and the one at the desk worked the scale.

Harry and I went to see Jimmy at his house to ask him for advice. It was the first time I had seen him since before going to jail. Jimmy was one of the biggest Cuban cocaine dealers in the Heights. I felt he needed to know what was going down in the event it had anything to do with this crew. I once heard the movie Carlito's Way was based on his story—not sure how true that was. He was a secretive guy, and when I was a youngster he would not deal with me because I grew up with his son. As an adult, he respected me and how I operated. He had heard that I held my own and became a stand-up guy. A lot of Italians came to his house and regularly hung out in front. As kids, we all knew he was well connected and nothing went down in this area without his knowledge. While I was away, I had heard of various shootouts when stickup kids would try to rob him at his house. He and his son were no joke. As soon as I told Jimmy about the guy I hit up in prison, he knew who it was. He told me the guy walked with a cane now and his face was disfigured. He said that it was his brother that was the big-shot in the family and had quite a few spots. He gave me their addresses along with the green light.

Harry already had the hardware we needed, so we started planning our mission. We sent someone to the first spot to make a buy, look around and report back the details. Once we received the particulars, we proceeded with the plan. We arrived separately to the buy house, not to raise any suspicion, but close enough to be taken up almost at the same time. While one of us was making the buy, the other walked in. The signal was when we made eye contact. As soon as we did, our guns came out. Harry got the drop on the guy at the scale and the one closest to him. I got the others. We zip-tied them, and bagged up the coke, money, jewelry, guns and anything else we could grab.

I left a message that said, "My name is Pepe. Tell your connection, it isn't over." We walked out of there without a struggle and went the opposite way to where our ride waited. We headed to our meeting spot. Once there, we split everything, paid the driver and put a cut on the side for Jimmy. His information was accurate. Now I knew the big connect's name, what he looked like, and what they call the piece of shit brother that put the contract on me.

We gave it a few days before we hit again. We moved on the same day the following week at a different location. After that, we switched up our days from Saturday to Sunday. We got together earlier in the day to review everything. Come sunset we were on our way. It was the same scenario. Again, we got the drop on them, and I left the same message. We got more money at the first spot than we did there but this time we got more coke, jewelry, and one weapon. We gave Jimmy most of the coke, the rest Harry put out on the streets. We sold the jewelry but kept the guns.

The following Sunday, we did the same thing, only this time we had to pistol whip one guy because he resisted. Again, I left a message, "My name is Pepe, tell your boss and his brother it's not over until the contract on me is off."

During this time, we kept a low profile. No clubbing or hanging out anywhere. I knew the Dominicans had to be looking for me. No one ever knew where I lived so I felt safe. That was the rule. I didn't hang near my place, and I stopped eating out and hanging at the local barbershop. A few of my friends got caught in a downtown restaurant and another at a barbershop, and were gunned down gangster style. I didn't want to take a chance, and I knew, word can get out fast when someone was paying the correct amount of money. I wasn't going out like that, so I needed to be smart. Things were relatively easy, but we expected it to get harder. They knew we would be back. The good thing is they had no idea when or how we would arrive. The element of surprise was always on our side. It was time to get ready for the next job. We scoped the action, the layout of the buildings and our route of escape at the next location. We prepared disguises, got our hardware and headed out.

As usual, someone took us upstairs. When we walked into the apartment, something didn't feel right. Guys were moving around unusually. Our plan was that if we felt something strange we would make the buy, keep it in hand and walk away. The signal was when Harry put the coke in his pocket. We bought a gram of cocaine. I tried getting his attention to see if he was seeing what I was, but he would not look at me. I wanted to call it off, when he decided to put it in his pocket. It was too late. We pulled out our guns at the same time, but this time there was a lot more pushback. Gunfire erupted on both sides. We didn't know that someone watched us through a hole in the other room all along. It was a setup. We got trapped in the room when all hell broke loose. I shot the guy behind the scale as he laid on the floor yelling for help. I tipped the desk so I could hide behind it and Harry used the wall. We spent a lot of rounds and still had to get to the front door before we ran out of bullets. We both spent a clip and only came with two each. There was no way to get to the front door without getting shot, but we needed to take that chance. I was not dying there.

The gun fire was heavy. You could smell the gunpowder in the air. Shotgun blasts were popping off like crazy from the guy in the next room. We picked up the guy that I shot and used him as a shield to get out. If they shot and killed him, at least it wasn't by us. To get out, we had to get the guy in the next room and the one at the hallway heading to the door. One guy already ran out, probably to get reinforcements. The hallway to the door seemed longer than before, and we had to get out of there before it was too late. We reloaded and decided to go for it using our live shield. I grabbed the guy; Harry got behind me and we made a dash for it. I focused on the guy in the next room. I began shooting through the wall; I heard the guy go down yelling and Harry got the one in the hallway entrance blocking our path. The guy had ran out of ammunition and dropped to his knees begging not to die. Harry shot him anyway. I was feeling a burn in my arm but paid it no mind. I let the one I held as a shield go because he was already hurt. We ran out of the apartment jumping a flight of stairs at a time while the adrenaline had us pumping in high gear. We exited the building with guns still drawn. We saw all the commotion then ran to the corner to our waiting ride. Harry scanned himself to see if he got hit, when he noticed the blood running down my arm—I had been shot. The bullet went through and out the other side. We got to the safe house, he took care of my wound, and we went over what just went down. They were prepared this time and had been waiting for us.

We had to change our approach. I turned to Harry and asked him if he wanted to quit. I let him know I would understand, but I had to see it through. Like a true soldier, he responded, "I'm with you till the end." The next day we took a ride over to Jimmy's house. We told him about the shootout. He wasn't surprised. They had been hit multiple times already.

Jimmy gave us the address to the Dominican brothers' main spot in the Bronx, where everything came in and got distributed from. We knew the spot would be well armed. It would not be easy. We decided to go on a stakeout. For a few days, we watched from a rooftop with binoculars. At one point, we doubted it was there because there was little to no movement. Of course, it wouldn't be like the other spots. It was a safe house for them and they needed to keep it on the low. We stayed there waiting and waiting to look for some type of routine. Then I saw him; the brother I stabbed in prison. He stepped out of a Lexus with a bag in his hand along with the guy I saw walking away from my table at the club the night the note was left for me. It was all coming together. Two hours later the guy from the club came out with some other guy I'd never seen before. They hung out at the building entrance and smoked a cigarette. Thirty minutes later they went back inside. When we were leaving, they all came out empty handed and got into the same car that drove up to pick them up. We learned what we needed to clean house.

Friday night. We drove through the block to scope the scene. Things were quiet. We made a second pass, got out of the car and walked around the block. We would enter the building, run up the stairs, and hide at the skyline until we saw or heard movement and then we would walk down and bum-rush. That was the plan. My heart was racing, I looked over at Harry, and without speaking, I knew his heart was racing too. As we were getting closer to the building, we saw the guy from the club with another guy going into the building. Harry wanted to abort the plan, at which time I told him this was a good opportunity. We kept walking and I told him the new plan. We decided to catch up and let them walk upstairs as we slowly crept up behind them as they got to the fifth floor where the stash house was at. When they knocked and the door opened we would rush them. What I didn't tell Harry was that if the guy saw us, he would recognize me, so I was planning to take him hostage up the stairs if that happened. I was not letting go of the opportunity and I wasn't turning back now—no matter what, this ends today. Fortunately, that didn't happen. All went according to plan.

The building had two sets of stairs going up on each corner. We took the opposite side listening carefully to the chatter and watching. They got in front of the door and knocked. When we heard the locks opening, we moved fast and got the drop on them as the door was opening. Holding onto the guys we rushed, we used them as shields as we made our way in. One guy came out to see what was going on, but ran back when we started shooting while pushing the three guys forward. One of them took off running, so I shot him, and we started going room to room for whoever was in there. Then someone began shooting from another room. One of the shields got hit and went down by their own guy. With the one guy we had left, we held him tight, and we began blasting off in the direction where the shots came from. I entered the room as Harry covered me. Behind the bed against the wall, there he was, the guy from prison with his arms in the air as he surrendered. He was telling me to take whatever we wanted.

He told me "There's the money and the drugs."

I slowly walked towards him holding my gun high and asked "Was this all worth it?"

He cried and told me, "It's all over, just take the stuff and you don't have to look over your shoulder anymore."

I pointed my gun to his head; he reached for his gun in a last attempt to live. I squeezed the trigger and watched him fall backward. "Now it's over," I said.

Harry and I grabbed what we had and on the way out he finished the last guy and said, "No witnesses." We quickly put on our masks, exited the building one at a time, and headed to our ride.

CHAPTER 9

Living the Life

Gangster.

With all the stuff that went down, I wasn't taking good care of myself. There was a cloud hanging over me that consumed me. Insomnia took over. I had too much on my mind, and I needed to unwind. Something had to give before I self-destructed. I decided to take a break to distract myself for a while. Harry and I chilled for a couple of months until the heat died down. We kept in touch with Jimmy and watched TV for any news. Harry knew some guy who drove a limo with O.J.'s Limo service. He gave him a call so we could get out a little and go downtown. Manhattan had this magic for making you feel better. I loved going downtown to the theaters, restaurants, and seeing people from all walks of life. It seemed like the whole world came there. It was just an electrifying atmosphere that would lift anyone's spirits. We played the clubs, did blow and drank, spending the money we got from the hits. It was a relief to be able to relax a little, but I still wasn't at ease. I wished it would all go away so I wouldn't have to worry any longer.

Clubbing became a regular thing. It was how I knew to de-stress. We enjoyed the new atmosphere and the sophisticated crowd. The women were gorgeous too. One night on our way to the club, we got pulled over. We were drinking and doing blow in the back of the limo. I got a little paranoid, and thought what if something came back to bite us in the ass? I was ready to reach for my gun. I was not going back to prison no matter what it took. He knocked on the window, told the driver to lower the glass and show him the car papers. We had the feeling by what he was saying that it was some bullshit; he saw a limo, decided to stop it and see how he can hustle us. It's not often you see a limo in the Heights, and with all the stuff going on there, he probably thought he would score. It was during this time that a lot of cops were on the take. They were on the payroll of some of the drugs lords in the area. Everyone was hustling in some form or another.

Soon after, shit hit the fan for a lot of cops. Corruption was at an all-time high and officers went down for all sorts of charges. They called them "The Dirty Thirty." It was the biggest police corruption bust to go down in the history of the Heights. Everyone had a price. It was the highest bidder for police protection. If you didn't pay, they'd take your money, your drugs and close you down. Then they would give your stash to whoever they were protecting for half the cost. Some dealers gave up other competitors so they could establish control. It was about who you knew, what you had, how powerful you were or how crazy you were willing to be. The movement was non-stop. Dealers and hustlers had to worry about the cops, the good ones and the bad ones, the stickup kids, and being ripped off by their own workers. Information was getting sold for cheap and bodies were showing up all over the place. Only the fittest survived. I knew I needed to slow things down. My life was on autopilot, and not going anywhere good. My paranoia was getting the best of me and I was always on guard. The tension was at its highest peak which made me uncomfortable. I kept a weapon on me at all times, even though I risked being pulled over and going back to prison, at the price of death it was something I had to do. It was not a life. I was jumpy and I didn't feel at peace at all.

Images of my life kept flashing in my mind. The little sleep I got was constantly interrupted by nightmares. Most nights I woke up in cold sweats. Spirits were haunting me. My dreams were crazy. It was always about some war, prison, fear or revenge. There were gunshots and me running all the time with no one around to help me. I was losing my mind. I was reliving the same things over and over again. I didn't like the unsettled way I felt. I lived my life with no meaning or purpose. I always had faith, but I lost my way. The void within was deep, and I needed to find my way back to civilization. I wanted to get back to when things were simpler. I needed my spirit to align with God in harmony. I couldn't take this any longer, and in desperation I broke down and asked for guidance. I was in a fog for far too long, and I needed to leave the game behind before there was a price I wasn't willing to pay.

Harry spent a lot of time locked up in his room. I wondered what the hell he was doing in there. When he did come out, he wouldn't make eye contact with me. I felt he was avoiding me and I became uncomfortable. I thought, "Maybe I overstayed my welcome." When our eyes locked on one another, I realized what he was doing all along was smoking crack. I was devastated and I wanted to beat his ass. I began packing that very day. I decided It was time to make a move. I was tired and had had enough. It would be the last time I saw Harry. A couple months later, I heard he got pinched and was doing ten years with the Feds.

I headed to the Bronx to stay with my younger sister Cindy, being that I let my place go. She had two baby girls with her. They were the cutest little girls. I enjoyed being there to look out for them. It was a quiet place to be. I took care of my sister and the girls, and she cooked to fatten me up. It was the much needed rest I was seeking. I kept a very low profile for almost two years. If I did go out, it was local, where little to no one knew me. Sometimes I would take a drive by the ocean to watch the sunset. Otherwise, I stayed at home to babysit my nieces. I found peace being home with family.

One day I came home to find Renzo, her daughters' father, sitting on the sofa bed that I slept on in the living room. I remember how shocked I had been when I opened that door and saw him. I hadn't seen him since the last time I went to see my son when he looked out the window, and we exchanged a few words. Now here he was. I couldn't believe my eyes. When I opened the door and saw him, I immediately stepped back out of the house and shut the door. I didn't know how to react, but I knew I was angry and that was not good. I opened the door again and rushed him. My sister was yelling and trying to separate us. She tried telling me that it wasn't what I thought and she kept apologizing. I just didn't want to hear it. I was too far gone by this time. We fought all the way out into the hallway. I threw him down a flight of stairs. In the lobby, I grabbed him by the hair and began banging his head into the mailboxes. He was hurt bad. He could barely put up his arms to fight. I kept punching him in the face until he turned into a pulp.

I began feeling sorry for him, and just as he was ready to go down I held him up, and I told him, "I loved you and you broke my heart." I left him and walked away back into the house.

My sister locked herself in her room. Days passed, and we didn't talk. I felt bad for what I did. I just couldn't understand why he would just show up there and think it would be alright. I felt violated by both my sister and him. It was as though neither one of them had any regard for my feelings or how big a deal this was to all of us. Our entire family was devastated by what he and my son's mother did. Everyone was affected by this including our friends. I wondered how my sister could do this to me after all the pain we had been through together. It was fine if she wanted to have some connection with him for the sake of the child, but she didn't have to drop it on me like that.

CHAPTER 10

The Disappearance

D ays went by and I hadn't seen my sister Cindy since she told me she'd be back, but that never happened. It was like she just vanished. Months had gone by without a word as to where she was. I was freaking out. I thought someone found out where I was and took revenge by kidnapping my sister. It scared the hell out of me. Or maybe she was still mad at me because of the argument we had the day Renzo showed up there.

I was unable to get a good night's sleep for days thinking about what could've happened to her. I jumped at every sound. I felt helpless and kept imagining the worst, like if someone kidnapped her, or even worse, killed her. I went through every piece of paper in that apartment, looking for clues. I went through her phone book, and called numbers I thought might be friends, but no one had heard from her.

I had to find my sister at whatever cost, but I couldn't do it with her daughters around. I needed to find a safe place for them where they would be comfortable in their mother's absence. I called my other sister Dee and had her take the girls. I didn't like them going from place to place, but I was powerless.

The phone rang one day. The voice on the other line was a woman. She sounded mysterious yet nervous. She said "I have some information about your sister, but we need to meet in secret without you telling anyone."

I said, "Yes, of course, where would you like to meet?"

"At the McDonalds' parking lot on Jerome at 3pm." she said. It was the first real lead I had.

I kept my composure because it could have been my only shot, so I needed to think clearly. It might even have been a set up. I didn't know what it was. I strapped down and got there two hours early in order to check out the area. Everything and everyone at this point were suspicious. While sitting in my car, I saw this girl approach. She appeared to be disguised. Something was going down, and I had to be very careful. I looked around as she approached. She did the same.

I got out of the car and her first words were, "Did anyone follow you? Did you tell anyone about our meeting?"

I told her no. She was frightened.

"This is a mistake, I shouldn't be here," she said as she tried to leave. I held her arm and reassured her it was going to be ok. She got into my car and we drove to the park down the street.

We sat on a park bench, and she told me something went down with some big-time Colombians. My sister had approached her and some other girls to recruit them for a deal. If they agreed, there was a big payday in it for them. If they traveled for the job, the pay was even bigger. They just had to escort some very important tourists around and make them look good. Everything was supposed to be safe.

She said, "We were all hyped about making twenty-five thousand dollars. There was three of us plus your sister. Later your sister told us that the plan had changed and we would have to take a trip for a day with all expenses paid. They would even give us some money to buy clothes so that we could look good. Your sister was upset because that wasn't what she expected. The deal for her was just to find the girls. Now she had to find a way to go too, or else she wouldn't get paid. When we got our passports, your sister called them. We didn't know where we were going before we left. The guy called and told us to take a cab to Queens and someone would pick us up there. This guy showed up in a limousine. None of us had ever been in a limo before. Something didn't feel right. We got nervous. The driver took us to Kennedy Airport, gave us some tickets for a flight to Miami and walked us as far as he could. Your sister went with us. She was really worried about leaving the kids but knew you would take care of them. When we landed at Miami Airport, we were greeted by someone holding up a sign with your sister's name and they directed us to another limo. By now, we were all impressed and felt important drinking champagne in the back of the limo. We drove to a marina, I remember it was a large boat with a name on the side that read *Key Largo*. We were greeted by an older guy in his forties I think. He told us there was a change in plans, and we needed to leave that night. We were scared. He took our passports, gave us some money, and told us to buy whatever we needed for an overnight stay. He told the driver to take us around, and meet in the hangar by 6 pm."

No Regrets

The girl paused and looked around before continuing. She told me none of them ever went to Miami before, let alone out of the city. She thought the limo guy who took them around was nice. They went shopping, laughed, and drank champagne. She thought everything was good. They wanted to talk but were afraid to say anything negative about the guy because he was always right there with them. She was scared that if they changed their minds about the trip, something bad would happen. They were taken to a private airport and got on a small red and white plane. When the man told them they were headed to Panama, they started freaking out. When they landed in Panama, a car was waiting. It took them to a large house where they got introduced to the men they were to escort. They had to follow their instructions, no questions asked. They were in a foreign country with no passport, money or even a phone to call home. Fear closed in on all of them when they were separated to go off with their respective "partners." Helplessness began to set in. She was told to stay at the house. It was getting late when she asked about my sister and the others. The man told her they would be back soon, but she never saw any of them again.

The older man she was with, told her he was a lawyer and they had some errands to take care of the next morning. He kept telling her everything was alright and to get some rest. The man never touched her, but she was still scared. She thought she would never see her kids again. She waited a little while until the man was sound asleep before she tiptoed out of the room and reached the front door then ran as fast as she could. She saw a wooded area and headed there running as fast as she could, going deep into the woods until she could no longer see the house. There she hid behind a tree until day break and started walking in fear through the forest when she saw a house in the far distance and headed there. She got to the front door and knocked. A man showed up, he saw the fear in her face, and in tears, she told him she needed help. The man let her in, they talked and he said he would do what he could to help her. She stayed with him and his wife a few months until they were able to get a passport and out of the country. Landing at JFK, she knew she couldn't go back home for fear the Colombians would come for her.

I thanked her for contacting me and promised I would do anything in my power to protect her. We got up to leave and then she asked me if I could stay with her for a while. I agreed. We went to where she was staying and talked half of the night. I felt her fear and was sorry that such a sweet innocent girl had to experience so much fear. Her life was forever changed over the promise of easy money. She asked me to lay down with her so she could hold onto me until she fell asleep. I was surprised, but said okay. She put her head on my chest, and a moment later we started kissing and then ended up having sex. In the morning, she made me breakfast. We talked some more before I left. After that, I never saw her again. She gave me a lot of information. I got the guy's name, description and probable locations. It was time for me to go on an adventure of my own.

CHAPTER 11

The Colombians, Costa Rica, & My Sister

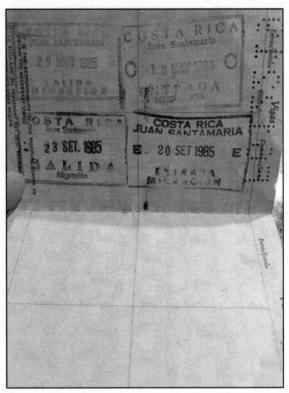

My passport after my trips to Costa Rica.

landed in Miami on a one-way ticket prepared to stay as long as it took me to get her back. I was traveling light in the event I had to get up and run quickly. If I needed anything I'd buy it as I went along. I took a taxi straight to the marina in search of a boat called *Key Largo*. I didn't know where the marina was so I trusted the cabby to get me there. After some time walking around and looking, I saw a boat that fit the description with the name *Key Largo* on the side coming into the marina. I waited and watched as it pulled into the dock. I felt anxious and my palms started to sweat. I began walking toward the boat when I saw someone cleaning it. I approached the guy and asked him for Joe. He was hesitant to answer. He asked, "Joe who?"

I gave him the description the girl gave me. He told me he didn't know who I was talking about and asked me who I was and what I wanted. I gave him my name and number. I told him I needed to speak to Joe about some very important business, and then I left. I knew by his reply I was on target, but it was no use asking any more questions.

I caught a taxi and checked into the Fontainebleau Hotel not far from the marina. This was where they filmed one of the scenes in Scarface. For four days, I went back and forth to the marina. I watched and waited from a distance to see any movement. There was none, the boat didn't move. I called for a taxi and headed to the nearest private airport in search of a red and white plane. There were a few planes there, so I checked them out one by one and left my number. There were some people near the last plane and I asked about the owner. They directed me to the hangar where the operations manager was. As soon as I walked in, one guy asked if I was there for a flight lesson.

I replied, "No, I am looking for Joe who uses that plane." He said, "I cannot give you that information, but if you like I can take your name and number and pass it on." I didn't expect anything different.

I already had my information with two contact numbers written down to give him. I hung around a while to watch for any action. There was none. I went for lunch, then back to the hotel. I checked with the front desk to see if there were any messages. The next day I hung around a while and decided that my business there was done. "Good thing I gave a second number." I thought. I caught a taxi to the airport and purchased a ticket back home. During the plane ride, I checked off what I accomplished and looked over what I still had to do.

I waited for a few days, but no one called. I headed to Queens in search of the limo that first picked up the girls. I was prepared for a long day. I knew it was not going to be easy. So far God was on my side. I prayed every day that he would keep me safe, and I would find my sister alive soon. It was six am when I got there. I circled every block within that area but saw nothing. I grabbed some lunch then headed back to the Bronx.

I was running out of options. The first day came and went. The second and third day as well. On the fourth day, the phone rang. The stranger's voice asked, "Are you Pepe?" I replied,

"This is him."

"You've knocked on a few doors looking for me, so here I am, what can I do for you?"

I told him, "My sister did some stuff for you and now she's missing. I'm only trying to find her and bring her back home to her children. Nothing more."

He asked, "Who's your sister?"

"Cindy, along with some other girls she got for you." I replied.

He said, "Okay, I'll tell you what. You got balls, and I respect that. Tomorrow at noon, be in Queens. There's a phone booth immediately after getting off the Triboro Bridge on the right-hand side at the corner on 29th Street and Hoyt Avenue, wait there, come alone, and if we see anyone else with you, you will never hear from me again. Agreed?"

I said, "Agreed."

I called my brother Jimbo and my cousin Mambo who just came home from prison.

"You guys be stationed a block away with a clear sight to this phone booth. Do not take your eyes off me. Look around, and see what else is going on. If I get into a car, take the tag. Don't follow me if you get the tag. If you don't get the tag, you follow but make sure to stay far behind," I told them.

No Regrets

The next day, I sent them with binoculars two hours before the meeting time to find a good parking spot. I got there a few minutes early in my own car so if they were watching they could see I was alone. I had to change my tags with the stolen ones I got the night before in case they tried tracing me. I was cautious to put nothing past these guys. I already knew they were heavy hitters, deeply connected. But I also could not show fear or intimidation. I made it clear my only motive was my sister. I parked the car and waited at the phone booth. Ten minutes past twelve a limo came speeding from around the corner and stopped in front. When the front door swung open, someone told me to jump in. The guy in the back seat told me not to turn around at any time. They took off pretty fast, turned the corner and continued zig-zagging through traffic. I hoped the guys got the tags because they were not going to catch up to this car without being noticed.

The first few minutes of our car ride were in total silence. They kept looking behind to make sure no one followed them. With the coast clear, Joe finally spoke, "So, you are Pepe, the guy that went through all that trouble to find me?"

I tried to relax but I was a bit occupied with the thought of getting a bullet to the back of my head. When I spoke, I intentionally turned quickly to grab a look at him, but he punched me in the side of the head and told me the next time I attempted to look back the outcome was going to be bad. I apologized but not before I got a glimpse of him. "I saw you mother fucker!" I thought. With my peripheral vision, I could see the driver well too.

Joe continued, "So you want to know about your sister? Well, she's locked up in Costa Rica. She got busted with one of our guys crossing the border from Panama with 25 kilos of our stuff. If she talks, she'll never make it out of there alive."

I told him, "If I can see my sister, I will make sure that she doesn't talk. I need your word that you will help get her out, and get her an attorney. I give you my word you will never have to see or worry about her again." He agreed. He told me the jail she was in, and said he would contact me. The car came to a stop.

He said, "Get out, walk and don't look back." I headed to my car, and drove to the Triboro Bridge back to the Bronx.

I called my brother, it was confirmed, they got the plate number. The following day I went to the post office to apply for my passport.

It took about six weeks before I received the passport. I booked the first flight to Costa Rica, and began packing. We landed in Costa Rica. I got my bag, walked to the money exchange booth, then took a taxi. I asked the cabby where there was a good hotel, and he took me to the Americana Hotel in San Jose. I checked in and went to the room to lay down for a minute. I showered, changed clothes to blend in with the locals, and then had dinner at the hotel. I was hoping to get around to do some sight-seeing before I left here. Afterwards, I went to bed. The next day, I would finally see my sister. After breakfast, I grabbed a taxi to the jail.

I stood in front of the jail, "El Buen Pastor." I walked in and noticed it was mostly run by male guards without uniforms. It made me uncomfortable. I checked in, and told them who I came to visit. A guard said, "La Americanita," and smiled at me. My sister was the only American there. Everyone only spoke Spanish and my sister knew very little Spanish. I was sure she was having a hard time. I waited and watched them operate. I saw how they searched others, and I wondered if I would be treated differently for being an American. I waited to be called. I was barely searched. They seemed to be only searching for weapons or something big. I knew what kind of jail this was and now I really worried about my sister. You could pass off anything in there.

To my surprise, I was escorted to the warden's office. He sat behind an old desk, and looked up as I walked in. He introduced himself to me in Spanish. He told me my sister was in a lot of trouble and faced 25 years to life for narcotics trafficking. The justice system in Costa Rica did not respond kindly to traffickers. He said that my sister was not being cooperative and therefore she would have a hard time completing her sentence." I didn't like the tone he used. I wanted to ask what he meant by her having a hard time, but I held back and listened. I wondered what the hell I was doing in the warden's office and what he had to do with her case. Things did not look good.

I thought maybe he was looking for a payoff so I asked, "What can I do to make her stay here safer?"

He replied, "I'll leave that up to you."

No Regrets

A letter to my sister in prison in Costa Rica.

I reached into my pocket and pulled out some money. I watched his eyes widen as I gave him five hundred American dollars. I asked when I would be able to see my sister. He called the guard in, and before I left, he said, "I don't want any trouble from you."

I was taken to the large visiting hall. There were other people there visiting prisoners. I looked around and noticed you could do whatever you wanted there because the guards didn't pay attention. I sat and waited for my sister. When she saw me, she ran and hugged me hard. We both started crying. She wouldn't let go of me. When we parted, I looked at her and my heart fell to pieces. She had lost a lot of weight. Her face looked drawn and tired. I saw the pain in her eyes. She was so happy to see me. She asked me how I knew where she was, and I told her about her friend and what I did to follow through. She became concerned for me and said, "Pepe, you don't know who you are dealing with." I assured her it was under control and how the guy was planning to help.

She began telling me about the bad experiences she had with the other girls because she was the only American. The other women in the jail, and even the guards kept trying to rape her. I wished I could have traded places with her. I was hurting so bad having to see my baby sister that way.

I tried hard to put up a front, so as not add to her sorrow, but I felt helpless. I wished I could have taken her home that instant and wash away all the pain. I asked if she could smuggle some money back inside. She said it would be no problem, so I passed her twenty one-hundred-dollar bills with ten twenties I had already prepared for her. I told her to pay her way off until she could win over some friends, and if needed, to pay off some guards to help her with whatever she needed.

Money was power in Costa Rica. One American dollar was worth thirty Costa Rican dollars and those guards couldn't have made much. Their lack of uniforms said a lot. They might not have even been guards, but locals that helped out at the jail. When my sister calmed down, I grilled her for the story. She apologized for all she put me through. She only did it because she didn't want to depend on me because I was doing too much already so she thought if she could do this and be safe, she would be back home the next day. She confirmed pretty much everything her friend had told me. She didn't know anything about what happened to the other girls until the guy arrested with her sent her a note through a guard from the men's jail nearby. It said, "Everyone got busted in different countries. I think we were the fall guys for a bigger shipment to get through. DO NOT TALK."

In telling her story, my sister said:

> They had my passport. I had no money and didn't know where I was or what to do. I got worried. They reassured me everything was going to be okay and the guy asked me to do him this one favor. I was only supposed to hang out with this guy and do nothing. We boarded this bus with a suitcase he was given. We were instructed not to open it. When we got across the border somebody would meet us, take the case and that would be it. We would turn around and come back home. I was really frightened. I didn't know what was in the case, but I had an idea. The guy I was with kept threatening my life if I said or did anything to create attention. I was afraid to look at anyone. The day before, at the room, he tried to rape me and I fought him off. The bus came to a stop on the border side of Costa Rica crossing Panama. The police got on the bus, looked around, came straight to the

back where we were seated, and then one cop asked for our papers. The guy had both his papers and mine and handed them over.

They asked, "Whose case is this?"

I froze and the guy immediately pointed to me. I told them it was his. We were then escorted off the bus and when they opened the case, I saw the drugs. I shouted, "That's not mine!"

She cried and told me:

"We were placed in handcuffs and my life turned upside down. I've felt lightheaded ever since. We were taken away in different cars to a jail where I stayed for three days. After that, they brought me here, and I've been stuck here, like in a bad dream. I knew this was a mistake but I let myself be driven by greed. My life is a living hell now. I hurt my kids and my family. Please help me get out of here I can't take it any longer, I miss my kids."

She sobbed for what seemed like forever. I reassured her that I would do all I could and that she wouldn't be alone. I thought of the movie "Midnight Express," and chills went up my spine. I remembered how the girl in the movie suffered and here I was witnessing the same thing.

She continued, "In a strange way, when I got caught it was a relief to be out from under that guy's control. He was constantly reminding me of what these people do to snitches. I was afraid. I don't know any Spanish, so I know I'm being manipulated here. They keep forcing me to take pills that keep me groggy. Some days I just want to kill myself."

I told her to hang in there, and she needed to stay strong. A guard announced that visits were over. She held onto me tightly and told me not to leave her. It was the most difficult moment for me. I told her I would be nearby and would stay around to see her again. Tears rolled down my face as I walked away.

On my way out, I asked to see the warden. A short time later, I was told that he was gone for the day. I took a taxi and headed to the American Embassy. I told the receptionist I was an American and asked to speak with someone regarding a family member's safety. I was taken to a room to wait.

A gentleman walked in, introduced himself, and asked me what he could do for me. He listened attentively as I began explaining the case, "My sister got arrested for trafficking narcotics across the border into Costa Rica. She is in a predominantly all male guard jail. There have been some rape attempts both by guards as well as the inmates. They have her on some drugs looking like a zombie. They force feed it to her. She is not very healthy and I fear for her life. I need your help." He empathized with me and then took my information. He said he would look into it and give me a call.

On the way back to the hotel, I notice I was being followed. I asked the cabby to make two left turns then a right. It was confirmed they were following me. I wasn't sure who was following me and why. I thought it was the warden's people who sent his goons to keep an eye on me. I was walking on a slippery road and had to be careful what I said or did. I wondered what connection there was with the warden and my sister's case. Why was he so concerned to make the statement he did—was he the judge and the jury as well? At some point, we lost the tail and we proceeded to the hotel. I had dinner at the hotel and then went to sleep.

The next day I went for a walk around town. I saw there was a lot of poverty. Costa Rica was a beautiful place, the people were very humble and always willing to help. When I got back to the hotel, there was a message from the embassy. I went to my room, picked up the phone and dialed the number. I was told that because of the serious nature of the crime, they couldn't do much for my sister. Therefore, they could not get involved. However, they could watch out for her safety and provide medical treatment. He told me to be careful because they didn't care for Americans here and if I needed anything else to give them a call. I thanked him and hung up.

I remember my oldest brother from my father's side had an ex-wife from Costa Rica with a son who lived here. I decided to give him a call. I got their number and I called. His ex-wife answered and they asked me to come by and stay with them. I checked out of the hotel and took a cab there. They welcomed me and treated me tremendously well. I met my nephews for the first time. She was worried about my safety so she decided to be my chaperone and show me Costa Rica. I hopped on the local bus to explore and headed towards the mountains where I saw the biggest volcano in the country. Here I was at the edge of this volcano looking into it. I have never seen one in person. It was amazing. Not many people were around, so I decided to go beyond the barrier rope to have a better look. I got so close, that at one point I slipped and fell, sliding closer to the edge. That frightened the crap out of me. I got outta there, mounted the bus and headed back. What a beautiful country. I woke up the next morning to a lovely day, and decided I was going to the beach. There I was on one of the most beautiful beaches I had ever seen. I found it unusual that there was no one in sight for miles. I got butt naked and ran into the water to be one with nature. It was like the beach was all mine. I laid in the sand, closed my eyes and thanked God for this moment. I stayed there and watched the sun as it set.

The following day I went back to visit my sister. When I saw her, she seemed more relaxed and happy. She told me that a doctor from the Embassy came to see her. He examined her and told her they would offer her medical care. Also, they had given her phone privileges. I told her about my visit to the Embassy. The visit was a pleasant one, so I decided not to share anything that would alter her mood. I was happy to see her in good spirits. It looked like she was making friends. She introduced me to some girls. That was a good sign. I was a little more relieved. Visiting hours were over. The last thing I told her was to be careful and to not trust anyone.

After visiting hours, I was escorted to the warden's office. He looked up from his desk and said, "I told you not to start any trouble. You are not to come back here and I recommend you leave this country at once for your safety and for your sister's."

I was dumbfounded by what he was saying. I got into a cab, and I called the American Embassy. They told me I was an American citizen and that anything that happened to me there would have repercussions, but they would not be able to provide safety for my sister or me. I told my sister-in-law, and she became concerned. I didn't want to jeopardize her or her family so I told them I was leaving. I picked up my things and headed for the air-port. Again, I was sure we were being followed. Only this time, I needed them to see me leaving.

I landed at JFK and went straight home to regroup. That night I got a call from my sister and I told her what happened with the warden. She had already heard because one of the guards that she befriended told her what went down. I advised her to be careful and extra cautious. I gave her our sister-in-law's number for any emergencies or if she needed something. At least now she had someone there for her and that gave me comfort. She informed me of her upcoming court date and was hoping that I could stay there with her but she understood. I told her not to worry and that I would take care of things from here. I told her I loved her and said goodbye.

Time passed and I didn't hear anything from the guy who got my sister into this mess. He promised he would call. It was 5am and I decided to take a trip to Queens in search of that limo. I started from the phone booth where I got picked up and went block by block. It wasn't until 7:30 am when I spotted a limo double parked on the street which looked similar to his. As I got closer, I saw that the tag was the same as what my brother had given me. I stayed back further down the street so I wouldn't be seen. I waited, and at 7:45 am I saw a lady with a kid come out from the two-story building as the driver got out to open the car door. It was the same driver I saw that day. I thought "How lucky can I get? Thank you, God."

The guy was probably on the payroll as a driver, and probably knew nothing but what he heard while driving. I followed the car. He stopped at a school where the kid was dropped off. Now I knew where his kid went to school. The car then returned to the same address, and the lady got out. The driver got out and opened the door for her and she went inside. Once the car left, I decided to get into the building. I looked up the names on the mailbox. I saw one with a Spanish name. I assumed it had to be them. I began picking the second entrance door lock, got in, went up the stairs to the door and listened. Everything was pretty quiet except running water possibly from the kitchen sink. I took a chance and knocked. She opened the door—it was the same lady. I introduced myself.

I told her, "I'm looking for Joe.

She asked, "My husband?"

"Yes," I replied.

"Are you a friend of his?" she asked.

"No, but it's urgent that I speak with him." I told her.

No Regrets

She let me in, directed me to the living room and asked me if I wanted some coffee. I looked around, and the first thing I saw was a picture on a fireplace. It was him. I told her the story of everything that happened without mentioning that it was her husband's fault or his 25 kilos. She was very sorry, but wasn't sure what it had to do with her husband. I told her that I was just here seeking his advice and his help because we were desperate. She told me that when he got back, she'd be sure to let him know. I left her my number and thanked her. Now I knew where he lived. Surely, he would call me.

No sooner than I got back, the phone rang. I recognized the voice. I answered, "How you doing, Joe?"

The tone of his voice had changed as he said, "I see that you like knocking on doors, only this time you've knocked on the wrong one. If you ever come near my family or my home again, I will make sure your sister, you and your entire family disappear."

I slowed him down and said, "Hey, I didn't hear from you and you gave me your word. My sister is not talking, and she has a court date coming up soon, so I needed to find you. I want to know if your word is any good, and if you're going to help her?"

He said, "I told you I would see what I can do, but never attempt to contact me again, or I will find you." He hung up.

I wasn't sure what else to do. Now I had finally acquired all this information and I wasn't able to do a damn thing. I didn't have the power to go up against this guy, and I wasn't able to protect my sister. I knew he was serious, and I understood because if someone came to my house where my family lived, I'd feel the same. I decided to let it go. Until I came up with some idea of how to use this, I was on my own. I booked a flight and headed back to Costa Rica with some money. I knew I would have to grease some palms.

I looked up an attorney who had told me he knew the judge and the district attorney personally, but it would take some money—as if I didn't expect that. I gave him my number to the hotel and headed out for lunch. I checked in with my sister-in-law and told her I was in the country. I explained to her that I needed to keep a low profile and so I could not go to the jail. She agreed to visit my sister and take care of things for me here. I felt truly blessed to have her there. The next day the attorney called me at the hotel and informed me about his conversation with the district attorney and judge. He told me it would take twenty thousand American dollars, and my sister would go free. I took a cab to his office to talk. He assured me that he would be able to take care of it. I gave him half the money up front and the other half when they came through. We shook hands and I left. Good thing I brought twenty grand with me plus a little more for spending. It was a good guess as to what most of these criminal attorneys would ask for. He knew I had people there, in case he thought of screwing me. I had no choice. My sister's court date was two days away, and I wanted to believe that she was coming home with me.

I got up very early that day and headed to the courthouse. My sister was the second case on the calendar. I sat through the first case and my anxiety level rose. I saw when she came out, my heart started to race as we looked at each other and smiled. The district attorney reviewed the seriousness of the crime. He stated that this charge carried a maximum of 25 years and the least they would offer was fifteen years. The judge spoke and asked my sister if she was prepared to plead guilty and take fifteen years. I could not believe what I was hearing. I was being railroaded. She looked at me in disbelief for some direction or signal. I shook my head as to tell her to say "No." She began crying, and I flipped out. I reassured her that I had this, and not to worry. Then she was taken away. The attorney was trying to hold me down and control me. I was trying to restrain myself from choking the shit out of him. He took me outside, and explained what happened, assuring me that he would talk to them. I told him he better get my money back, if not it wasn't going to be pretty.

I waited around all afternoon. The lawyer came back and he told me that the judge and the DA learned that there were more people involved and how some other girls got busted in Mexico. He said other people were asking questions, so they had to be careful. If they were to take this big there was a risk it would cost me another five grand, and the best they could do was five years, and they needed it up front. I was being scammed. I felt powerless. Who is to say if I agree this won't happen again? Damn criminals! Before I punched this asshole in the face and got locked up myself, I stormed out of there and headed to a local bar. I came back when I was a little calmer and I told him that I needed some reassurance this time because

No Regrets

I knew they were scamming me. He told me not to worry that he'd get it done, and if not he'd get me the money back. He said he would call me when he got any news. I decided to hang around the court and watch the attorney as he left and follow him home. I wasn't going to be had that easy.

I went back to the bar to de-stress. There I met a woman. We talked, had a few drinks then we both went back to the hotel. I wanted to drown and numb my pain away. We had sex, then she left. I had no choice. I needed to take the risk, but I didn't have the full amount with me. I called the attorney and asked him for an account to wire the money. He kept trying to justify the scale of the case but assured me everything would be okay. I flat out told him it better and warned him not to screw with me. I called the airport and booked a flight back home. I went directly to the bank where I had my safe deposit box and immediately wired fifteen thousand dollars. The thought was premature, but I was thinking about how I would get even with them all if they screwed me again. Three weeks later, she had a mysterious court date that no one knew anything about. There she was sentenced to five years.

She and I talked as I assured her it would be ok and not to worry about anything back home and that I would take care of everything. She said okay, thanked me and told me she would be fine. In her voice, I felt she was telling me the truth. This gave me great comfort. My sister-in-law was a great support. She promised to be there to do all she could. Six months later my sister told me the jail was now run by Nuns. It was the best news I heard all year. I guess maybe going there and making noise paid off.

CHAPTER 12

Seville
& the Downfall

Gangster with a gun.

The next few years were pretty rough for me. My mom's health and state of mind kept declining. She had been suffering for a while from a stroke which left her paralyzed. Ever since Pop died a few years before, Mom hadn't been the same. You could tell she was lonely without her companion of forty plus years. Although he had his drinking problem, he loved my mom, and now with him gone, all her kids grown living their own lives, losing her apartment and now having strangers caring for her, she became lonely and felt like she had no reason to live. I saw the pain in her eyes as she zoned out and got lost in some thought or another world she never came back from. My brother had to bathe her when the home attendant wasn't around and that embarrassed her. She felt ashamed, humiliated and powerless. I felt really bad for her. I'm not sure I could've done that, and even the thought of it made me queasy.

I asked her how she felt one day, and she replied, "I want to die." I cried, she cried. The only thing I could do was hug her because I understood her pain. Here she was, in a tiny strange room in a different borough with a TV and a hospital bed that she couldn't get out of when she wanted. She would lay there and stare at the ceiling as the walls closed in on her. She felt hopeless. There was nothing left for her. She told me about an insurance policy she left for me, and at that point, I knew she was serious about checking out. For the very first time, words had escaped me as I stood there, hugging her to provide whatever comfort a child could give to his mother. My heart ripped apart as I left there saddened. Lost in emotion, my head spun. I felt like I was in another world. I couldn't take the pain and walked outside. I sat on the stoop and cried. That was the last time I saw her conscious. She fell into a coma and never came out of it. Two weeks later my mother died. I think she gave up and was trying to prepare me for it. My life forever changed on many levels. Her death hit me the hardest.

My siblings and I got together to discuss how we would tell our sister Cindy, who was still in a Costa Rican jail cell. Since she was already suicidal and destitute in a foreign country by herself, we didn't think that she would be able to handle the news. I made the decision not to tell her. Months passed, and when she called asking for mom, we made excuses, either she was sleeping, not feeling good, at an appointment or with the home attendant. After a while, she found it suspicious and didn't accept the excuses any more. She knew something was wrong and wanted to know the truth. It was my brother's wife who gave in and told her what happened. As I suspected, she didn't handle it well. I spent a lot of time calling the institution over there trying to talk with her. They told me that she was on medication that kept her sleepy. I left messages for her to call me when she could, but she never did.

Some months passed when I finally heard from her. She was very hurt and angry at me for depriving her of the right to know about Mom's passing. She refused to accept my apology and didn't talk to me for some time. I lived with the decision I made for a very long time as my heart ripped to shreds. It was one thing I always wished I would have done differently.

I took to hanging with my cousin Mambo. He was one crazy guy. We ran around the Bronx, where everybody knew his name. He was a good salsa dancer—that's how he got his name. He used to run with some big players. He had mad respect on the streets. Plenty of people feared him and plenty more wanted him dead. I was known a little as well. I also had a little respect and was known as Pepe Seville. People identified me with the Cadillac Seville I drove and the name stuck. The saying was, "There goes Mambo and Seville, the brothers; if you do one, you have to do the other."

He sucked me back into the game that I had been fighting so hard to stay out of. This time the stakes were higher. As two felons getting together, our imaginations ran wild. If we had gotten caught doing some crime, we would go up the river for a good while. We began running the streets, doing dirt and getting high. I had been shot twice in my own battles, but it seemed like Mambo had nine lives. He had bullet holes all over his body and had survived them all. He was walking around with only one kidney due to a shot that ripped his stomach out. He had a girlfriend in Spanish Harlem, named Marleen. She worked at Harlem Hospital where they met when he came in for another gun shot. She lived in the Jefferson Housing Projects on Lexington and 112th St.

No Regrets

Me and Mambo.

I loved Marleen. She and I got real tight. I spent many days hanging at her house. One day at Marleen's house, Mambo and I stepped out to buy some dope. I was in my early thirties the very first time I ever tried snorting dope. When I was putting dope out on the streets, we would cut it to make more, than we'd give it to someone to sample it by shooting it up, then tell us if it was any good. One time, I thought the guy was lying when he said the dope was weak. Some would say that just to get more for free. So to see if he was telling the truth, I decided to find out for myself, and I snorted some. I remember throwing up all over the place and hating it. I wanted to kick his ass for lying. What I remember, was how it took away my back pain, which I was having a lot of problems with. I had a lot of respect for heroin, and I saw first-hand what it did to others. It became your whole life once you allowed it to sink its white teeth into your system.

My plan was to use it only when I was in pain, and be sure to not do three days in a row so I wouldn't get hooked. I started liking how it made me feel. It was like a super-duper tranquilizer, and like magic, it took all my troubles away. It was my escape from reality, but the escape didn't last long, and I found myself using it every day in order to feel good. I didn't see it as a problem because I had money and plenty of dope available, but after using it for a while, it began to possess me and I became obsessed with it. This was when the problems began. My whole disposition and attitude changed. I turned into Jekyll and Hyde, and now needed the drug just to feel normal. Although it happened over time, things began going downhill from there.

Once, Mambo and I walked into this hallway on 109th Street, and as soon as the guys saw us, the commotion started and the guns came out; shots were being fired at us. I yelled "Hold it, hold it; what the fuck is going on?" While hiding behind a little piece of wall protecting us from the gunfire near the exit door to the street. I kept yelling "Stop it, stop it," as we tried to decide when to run out. I don't know how we made it out of there without getting hit, but to save our lives, we had to run out and jump head first over a parked car while the gunfire rang out. We were trapped, and if it weren't for a police car passing by, we would've been dead. It was the first time we were happy to see the police. The cops noticed Mambo had been shot in the legs, so he was rushed to Harlem Hospital. He became a danger to hang out with. He'd done so many people wrong that I never knew if they were gunning for him or for me. We never found out why they shot at us, but I assumed, it was someone he'd done wrong. We thought about going back to take care of business once Mambo got better.

My life was spiraling out of control. I woke up one day not feeling well. I thought I was coming down with a cold and decided to stay in bed. As the day progressed, I became worse.

Mambo called me, "Bro, what you doing?"

I told him, "I'm in bed feeling like shit."

"When was the last time you did some dope," he asked.

"Early yesterday morning," I answered.

"Bro, you're dope sick," he said. "I'll be right over."

It was about 5pm and I was still in bed shivering, sweating a river - yet ice cold, runny-nose, and cramping. When he came over, he took out a bag of dope and handed it to me. I opened the bag, and at the first sniff, I immediately felt better—I was hooked on this shit! Why in the hell did I start messing with this stuff! This is what my life had become!

Afraid of running out of money, I began to invest in larger quantities of heroin to put on the streets. I had three spots; one on 184th and Morris

Avenue, the other on 184th Street and Briggs and one in Newark, New Jersey. My life got consumed with the hustling. I needed it to stay alive, support my habit and remain in the game. It was time-consuming: the getting, cutting, bagging, stamping, and finding others to sell it. I found the cheapest laborers—crack addicts. After a few days of doing alright, they would take off. What did I expect? I spent more time looking for them in crack houses then I was operating the business. It was a disaster. I closed shop in the Bronx and stuck with New Jersey, where I was getting $12 a bag. But when the guy who previously controlled this spot came out of jail demanding a cut, we began to have problems. We had a territorial fist-fight, but when I fucked him up, he couldn't deal with it and came back with the longest handgun I had ever seen—some shit from the "Wild, Wild West." He chased us out, and that was the end of New Jersey. Now I was fucked.

I needed product fast and my money was low, so I contacted my Colombian cocaine connection I met in the joint. At that time, the Colombians began exploring with heroin because the payoff was bigger than coke. I took a trip to Queens to see him. He hit me off with a few ounces of some heroin. It was so weak, I couldn't cut the shit, and even at its purest form, nobody wanted it. I called him back to return the stuff, before I really fucked this up and I ended up with a "Colombian Necktie." As it was, I had to explain why a good portion was gone. The truth was that because it was so weak, we had to keep experimenting and giving out samples. He had to have known this product was trash and thought he could pass it off to some fool. I placed my gun in the back of my pants as I waited for their arrival. I heard the knock at the door and got up to open it. We sat down and I began telling them what was going on and how I felt. They were heated when I told them this, and at that point I began worrying as the other person with him began staring me down with that certain look, letting me know I fucked up. Reluctantly, he took his product back, and after saying a bunch of shit to me, he let me off the hook, and that was the end of our relationship. What a relief that was—I thought they were gonna try to kill me. When they left, I pulled out my gun, sat down, and with the gun at my side, I said to myself, "I can't keep doing this."

I was becoming desperate, so I went to see one of the biggest connections in the Bronx who Harry and I knew. On our reputation, he hit me off free of charge with an ounce of pure so that I could get on my feet. This was going to put me on again. I put it out on the streets, but there was better shit out there so my stuff wasn't moving as well; it wasn't the same quality stuff their brand was made of; so he gave me some other shit. "What is wrong with these dudes?" I said, "They give out the shit others give them that they can't move." I was pissed. It was my last shot and I failed.

The money was low. My energy was spent on getting, using and finding more means to get drugs. I was down to my ride and my name, and soon, even that didn't carry any weight. I began sticking up the other dope spots to support my habit, until I couldn't even walk onto a block without people already knowing who I was and giving me a hard time. I lost everything. I hit a low and became ashamed of myself, and now I had this monkey on my back. Man, how far can pride go down? I tried to get off by cutting down my using, but that got difficult as hell. I couldn't deal with the symptoms of kicking the habit, but I wanted and needed to stop. Everything in my existence now depended on heroin. I'd go to bed thinking about the stuff and wake up thinking about it. Nothing else mattered except the next one; even life and family took a back seat. I knew that with help, I could get that stuff out of my system, but only some kind of god would be able to get it out of my soul and mind. I was no longer me!

I lost the apartment that once belonged to my sister before she got busted, and I was now homeless. I didn't want to burden anyone in my family or have them see me like this. I spent many nights sleeping in my car or looking for some woman I could hustle a meal, a shower, and a place to sleep, in exchange for sex. I didn't always like some of the places I'd wake up at, but that was the price I had to pay. I was a male prostitute, and I sold my soul to the devil for cheap.

One time I went home with this woman and stayed there the entire weekend. Even when I was tired, all she wanted to do was screw all day long, every waking moment, while I just wanted to nod and mellow out. I wasn't as attracted to her and she was becoming annoying. Come Monday she left me sleeping and went to work. I had planned not to be there when she got back. I took a shower, had a meal, then proceeded to leave. When I got to the door, I realized she had a two-key cylinder lock and all the windows had gates with locks on them. I searched for keys, but found none. I looked for tools to break the locks, but there were none. I was trapped and it terrified me. I needed to get a fix! I became a sex slave at the mercy of a woman I didn't know. It was not how I envisioned things. I hit another low. I was riddled with guilt and shame. I watched some TV, and waited till she got back for what seemed like forever. She locked the door behind her with the keys, as I watched her place them in her bag. I was cordial and acted as if everything was alright. I told her I was going to the store, she took the keys out and unlocked the lock. I went up the block to cop some dope and I never came back.

One day my brother-in-law Sal and I, went for a ride to buy some dope. I was a dollar short and the dealer wouldn't give me a bag for the money I had. I flipped out. I went to my double-parked car, pulled out an Uzi and began waving it at the entire block. Everyone scattered. People screamed and ran into the building. I noticed the connection watched what was going down. He also turned and ran into a building. I ran toward him and chased him up the stairs. I saw him go into an apartment, so I banged down the door. His wife opened the door and cried in fear.

She begged, "Please, please don't hurt us. I have kids here."

I told her "Tell him to come out or I will go in and get him."

He came out with drugs in his hand and said "Here, take it but leave my family alone please."

I told him, "That's not what I'm here for. I am here because of the lack of respect. You know who I am out here yet you chose to disrespect me." He apologized to me and gave me some dope. I snatched the dope from his hand and took off. I opened a few bags and snorted the dope before I left the building.

I got in my car then noticed the cops, they were after me. Sal began panicking. Someone had snitched on me. I sped up Morris Avenue, and a car pursuit ensued. We lowered the windows and as soon as we turned the corner he threw his gun out and I did the same, but the cops found them both. I rode on sidewalks to get around the roadblocks. Finally, I came to a dead stop near the school yard on Creston Avenue. I jumped out of the car, threw my hands in the air and got on the ground. We were both handcuffed, but I was the one being kicked in the face, head, chest, ribs and hit in the head with the baton. While in the patrol car, the officer continued to hit me across the face and head. I fell in and out of consciousness as he hit me again and pulled me back up to do it over again. I looked so bad while in the bullpen, my brother-in-law put my head on his lap to comfort me. Blood was everywhere. The paramedics came and patched me together. It wasn't until I got to the jail that they realized I was still bleeding and they stitched me up. I was placed in Bronx County Jail. I was hurt so bad I couldn't see out of either eye and needed an escort in the jail to walk me around.

Jail.

Not only was I in pain from the cop's ass-whipping, but the next day I was beginning to get dope sick. I was in a living hell. I had the shits, vomiting, cold sweats—all those terrible symptoms came back—a hundredfold. There are no words to describe what I was going through, but I knew I wanted to die, and that's what I thought was happening. After three days, I began feeling a little better, but I was still very weak. God did for me what I couldn't do for myself; he saved my life—***no mas***—never again! Dying is easier than this! I was happy I was in jail and out of the reach of a dope bag.

This was my bottom. I hit an all-time low. How did I ever get to this? I terrorized a family and did all of this because of respect that I lost—all due to my fault. My image had been shattered. No one had any respect or fear for me any longer and I felt terrible.

I learned the arresting officer from the local precinct in the Bronx was Detective Frank Lavoti, the same cop that in 1994 put a chokehold and killed a kid named Anthony Baez after a football hit his patrol car's windshield. He was brought to trial and later found guilty of murder. He was sentenced to fifteen years in jail, and even other cops went down for trying to cover up the story. When I got better, I proceeded to start a lawsuit against him and the police department for my excessive beating. No lawyer would take the case being that I was already locked up. So, not only did I surrender my freedom once again, but was at risk of going blind. This guy should never have been a cop, and the only restitution I got was that he got convicted and his career went to hell. I can't remember a time when I got arrested, that the cop didn't kick the shit out of me or busted my head open with a six-battery flashlight.

I put on a little weight in prison and I was doing better. I heard from family that my sister got freed from jail in Costa Rica. She and my son Anthony visited me in jail. It was tough. I pretended to be okay but, deep down inside I was hurting. I was ashamed. I felt like a loser. Now she was trying to make me feel better. I felt conflicted. I was happy it was a short visit. Before leaving, I told her never to visit me there again. I went back to my cell and cried like a baby. The thing I had wanted most was to welcome her home one day, not to have her visit me in jail.

I took a plea and was sentenced to a 2 to 4 year term and was shipped upstate to begin my time. This time was different because it almost felt like I was being rescued. I was really tired—my butt was whipped. I was shipped off to Altona Correctional Facility. There I played softball to occupy my mind. I attended my first Narcotics Anonymous meeting. I know I needed to take a hard look at myself and I was ready to work at it. I also attended a class with the Alcoholic Substance Abuse Program (ASAP) that addressed addiction and recovery issues. After some months there, the civilian counselor liked me and asked me if I'd come work with him in the class as his counselor assistant. He put in a referral and that became my jailhouse job. Just when things were getting good, without me having a clue, I got shipped out—that really pissed me off. I ended up in Washington Correctional Facility, where not even the COs had control, and didn't care. I tried hard to keep my cool and stay away from all the jailhouse bullshit. All they talked about was the big one, or getting a package once they got out and flipping it. I had been down that road too many times, and I knew, it was a dead dream with no happy ending; the results were always the same—"jail, institutions, or death." Very few guys ever actually quit the game to go on and live happy, joyous and free on some remote island drinking gin and tonic. It was all an illusion, a fantasy. The game itself was an addiction and most people played it for life or until death.

Freedom.

I got paroled on good behavior after two years. It was 1991. By now, at 33, I had spent over a third of my life in and out of jails and institutions. Although it felt great being released, I was concerned with where was I going now, as I would be homeless once again. I called my younger sister Cindy, and thankfully, I was able to stay with her and her new husband for a while. They even welcomed me with a big Puerto Rican feast with family and friends. We had rice, beans, steak, and salad, which made me feel so good—how I missed that.

I looked up a few of my boys, got hit off with some loot and was able to put a deposit on an apartment in Pelham Parkway in the Bronx. I took the lease to the welfare department and they helped me maintain it. It was a one-bedroom and pretty spacious, probably too much space for the nothing I had. I found me a used bed frame for cheap and purchased some low-end mattress and I was good. It definitely beat being in jail. Everything else would come with time. I bought a motorcycle which became my new means of transportation and began making NA meetings. I was doing alright. I got a job in the garment district selling ladies apparel. I started traveling, doing the fashion show from Las Vegas to Miami and in between. It didn't pay much, but with the commission on sales, it wasn't bad. When I wasn't doing a show, I'd be at the store. I was always a smooth talker, so it made me a good salesman, and when I was high, man, I could talk some game; there wasn't anything I couldn't sell.

I was still suffering with my back pain and all the traveling with work. After about a year of being clean, I had to go meet a friend in the hood who was locked up with me. Being so close to the block, of course, I couldn't resist walking through there just to see what was going on. I ran into some of the old crew from the block that used to sell dope and they were getting ready to put out samples of some new stuff they got. I ended up hanging out for a little too long, all the while being tempted to know just how good the product was. My spirit was telling me to go, but my mind kept me hostage. I knew I shouldn't have, but I couldn't resist the curiosity. Fighting an internal battle, I continued to rationalize my staying, until finally I was exhausted and surrendered to my desires. I reached my hand out for one of the samples. In recovery, there's a saying "Stay away from people, places, and things that you associate with your addiction. It was the one suggestion I didn't take, and again I paid the price.

Suddenly, I was right back where I left off! All that time the gorilla was still inside my mind, sitting and waiting for the opportunity to break out. I hated myself for being so weak, yet again. My spirit was fading and that same old lost feeling surfaced, I was back to beating my own ass, and for the next six years, I was on a run.

Four buildings joined in a courtyard where I lived, all connected through the basement where they had the laundry machines. That's where I first met Yolanda. Soon after, we started dating, and it wasn't long before we shacked up together. Again, I didn't let go of my place—just in case. And when I needed some time alone, that's where I went. At the beginning my using was not bad. I was able to maintain my job and be responsible, but as time went by, going to get some dope before work was important, and that's when I started showing up late. They tolerated more than usual because I was their best salesman but gave me a lot of shit. Soon I was calling out sick more frequently until I just stopped showing up. Now, I was just hustling whatever I could here and there to stay afloat.

Yolanda had an idea that something was wrong because my whole demeanor had changed, but she had no clue it was because of drugs. Then one day I confessed and told her I needed help. She agreed to do whatever she could and continued supporting me, but had no idea how to help. After experiencing the shame, guilt, and a world of pain, I came to the conclusion that this game was no longer for me. I was afraid that I'd find myself again in a prison for a much longer time, and again thinking about committing suicide, I knew this time I wouldn't be able to handle another bid. I really needed to change, something had to give, but what would I do, and how would I do it this time?

I kept experiencing the same feeling every time I'd fuck up, and the guilt got worst. I found myself on my knees praying for God to just take me and get it over with. The following day while getting the mail, I opened up a letter addressed to me from a credit card company that read: "Here is your new card with a maximum limit of $3,000." I didn't remember ever applying for a credit card and I don't know how it happened, except that I felt there was a divine power at work here. I stood there while looking at this card in my hand, checking the name over again for any mistake, but there was none; it was my name. The very first thought that came to my mind was a commercial I saw about a procedure to detox from heroin within 24 hours for the low cost of $3,000. Immediately, I knew what I had to do.

I told my girl what happened. I found the paper where I wrote down the commercial information while watching TV. She picked up the phone and the following day we had an appointment to go to Connecticut and make me new. I was desperate and willing to try anything to avoid going through the withdrawals, so I headed there for an intake and was accepted on the spot.

Three hours into the process, I went into convulsions and almost died. I fell into a coma while under anesthesia. It was so bad the whole procedure had to be stopped. I remember feeling I was drowning in a lake of ice and I couldn't break through to stick my head out. I was suffocating on my saliva. It was as though I was in a long dream watching myself dying and I couldn't wake up. My brain kept saying "Wake up, wake up," but my body was paralyzed. Just before I knew I would die, I took that last gasp of air and woke up terrified. I was in shock. Fortunately, the doctor was able to regulate me, as I laid there helpless in a comatose state. It took a few days to come to my senses. I was feeling extremely exhausted and unable to move, while all along I was shitting and vomiting all over the place throughout the day and night. I was still detoxing. It was a living nightmare. Poor Yolanda. She stayed with me throughout this whole process, sleeping in the clinic bed next to me, cleaning up all this crap in the middle of the night behind me. I know she suffered and felt helpless. After a few days, she took me home and nursed me back to health. She stood by my side and supported me; she was so good to me.

It took four months to get my strength back before I was able to leave the house for a walk. It was an experience I'll never forget, and one I could never go through again and survive. This time it was for real—"no mas!"

On August 8, 1998, I walked into my first Narcotics Anonymous meeting back from the relapse to surrender and dedicate my life to the healing of my spirit. It hadn't come without a price, and things were not easy, but it was the challenge and struggle I needed to get through to learn what I have. I didn't want to die, and I was tired of suffering. I had the will in me all along, I just needed to dig deeper and trust that my God would not let me down if I found that reason to want to live. I now have a better understanding of what life is all about, and the things one must do to obtain and keep freedom.

I was so grateful to Yolanda who cared for me and helped nurse me back to life. I put her through so much and couldn't have done it without her. She was one of the great women in my life. For most of my life, I've been pretty independent, but it felt good having someone take care of me. We fell hard for one another and got along well. There was a lot of passion and plenty of great sex. However, I was still feeling that familiar void. I felt incomplete. I remember, every time I got personal and let someone in, I always had the same reaction, and a feeling of wanting to run. I'm still trying to figure out if it's fear of revelation, issues with abandonment or if I'm just a lousy dude. I tended to become tired pretty quickly, which explains why most of my relationships were short. It was unfair to the women because while they were getting involved deeper, my mind was already checking out. I broke a lot of hearts.

Yolanda's young son was making things a little difficult for me. We kept banging heads. I didn't realize he was just a jealous kid, and since it was always the two of them, I was an intruder. I tried ignoring all this noise, but I wasn't that good at getting it out of my mind. Deep inside, I knew I needed to go. We were crazy about each other, and that was making this even harder. My conscience kept telling me in a very calm tone that this was not for me, and, again, I ended up hurting another woman. **For the first time, I began to feel the pain that she was feeling and it was killing me within.**

The day came when I mustered up the courage to be honest. When she got home from work, I told her I couldn't do this any longer. It broke my heart as I saw the shock and pain in her eyes. She didn't deserve this. She was a wonderful woman. It felt as if I stabbed myself in the chest over again. I wasn't sure what I'd done, and for a moment wanted to take it all back, but it was too late, the decision was made. I was sure this was not what I needed, and if I invested more of my time I may get stuck here. The thoughts haunted me for a while as I struggled with my conscience. In the end, it was the best decision I made. I needed to move on, it just didn't feel right anymore.

I went back to my apartment. Months went by, but we remained friends and looked out for one another. She even got me a job at a porn distribution company where she was the bookkeeper. I started as a salesman and one day I was even able to direct some of the movies. We hung out here and there. For me, it was more about sexual gratification, but for her, I knew she still loved me, and if I continued this, it would only hurt her more. I decided to put an end to everything, even though seeing her at work was not easy. We tried to be professional when we crossed paths, but I could still feel her pain. I had to leave and find another job. I couldn't keep hurting her this way. By this time I was feeling strong enough and I knew I would be alright on my own. She helped me on the path which would eventually lead me to begin to change my life.

Eventually, I ended up quitting the job and moving on. Some time later, when she knew it was over between us, she got into an abusive relationship with some jerk. Years later I wanted to see how she was doing and I went looking for her. She was no longer living at the same place, so I went to her cousin's house to look for her. She gave me the news that her boyfriend had shot her seven times killing her, shot himself, and then set the house on fire. I was devastated. I stood there in shock as a tear rolled down my face. For days, the thought of her death was so disturbing, I couldn't shake it. I went to the library to look up the article and there it was— just like her cousin had said. I couldn't believe it. Death had never touched me this close and for months I grieved. She was such a good-hearted person, and her memory will be with me forever.

Many years later, after coming out of the military, her grown son called me. We talked and he asked me to forgive him for chasing me away. He said, "My mother loved you, and you were the best thing for her and I chased you away; I am so sorry, this would've never happened had you stayed with her."

I apologized to him for not understanding that he was just a kid who wanted his mother and that I was the intruder. We both cried, and said we missed her.

CHAPTER 13

Finding Me

A As I continued on my journey, I became more aware of my patterns, and what I had done over and over my entire life. I was always seeking power and fulfillment in order to feel complete.

I became attracted to needy women who empathized with me. I always made sure they had their own apartment; this way we didn't have to become that deep, and I'd always be able to go back to my own home. It was important not to let them know too much about me and my story, but just enough so that I could keep them where I needed them. In most cases, I knew how this would end, because for me, women were a mere stepping stone. However, I did have compassion and love in the process. Many times I tried to change my original way of thinking but my relationships always ended. I knew there was an issue with my behavior and attitude toward women. Some of them I really dug and thought I could make a life with them, but my lack of trust, and fear of letting someone in, were more powerful than the emotion of love. Because of my inability to stay and fight, or get help; running became much easier, so nothing ever lasted. I abandoned everyone and everything I was sure of when things got too intimate, and retreated to that familiar place I was so comfortable at. This was pretty much the pattern of my life. Relationships were just a means to an end. I looked at women as objects, and most times, I used sex as a weapon for control. Fulfillment was always around the corner or confined to short-lived pleasures. I thought the higher the thrill, excitement or sex, the more fulfilled and complete I'd become.

My goal was to obtain wealth, and indulge in all worldly things to give meaning to my life. It was always about the obsession, getting somewhere in the future, using things and people as an escape, because I was unsatisfied with who I was. It was like a repetitive script in my mind that gave me identity, but distorted and covered up the real story of my life.

I didn't want to keep going in circles with this for the remaining part of my life. I decided to take a hard look at myself. Having been financially well-off, and having been with some of the prettiest women, I knew none of it had a lasting effect. Everything up to this point was always about instant gratification, and now I felt there was more about me that I needed to uncover. I started by reminding myself that nothing outside of me could fill the void, and that I had to get down to the reasons why I was always ending up at the same place within. Breaking this cycle was not going to be easy, but I was willing to begin learning about me. For sure, I wanted to find stability, and of course some peace; so my quest for self-discovery began, and I decided to remain alone for a while.

I learned to be grateful for the small things—to breathe, and to just be alright with who I am, despite the flaws and the pain I had inflicted on myself, and no matter what the current situation was in my life, whether joy or pain, I slowly learned to take the time to smile and laugh with life. I was alive… and not in a jail cell... It was now time to take charge, put the pieces of my life back together and begin living a new life. I was feeling better and more confident. I finally believed everything was going to be alright. I grew stronger by the day and began planning out my future. I often thought maybe I had to go through this whole mess to bring me closer to finding my life's meaning and purpose.

CHAPTER 14

The Resurrection

t was the spring of 1999. One day while running on Orchard Beach I saw the most beautiful woman. Something drew me to keep looking her way. She was so fine, I couldn't take my eyes off her while she laid there tanning. After my jog, two hours later, I saw she was still there, so I began walking in her direction hoping she would notice me, and as I got closer, I said, "Do you need help reaching your back with the tanning lotion?"

She said, "No, I got it."

I asked, "What's your name?"

She said, "My name is Sky."

We stayed there talking for hours and when it was time to go, she asked me, "What are you doing tonight? Would you like to go with me to an event my girlfriend is having?"

I knew I didn't have any plans and said "Yes, of course, I'd love to." We said goodbye and as I walked away, I couldn't contain my excitement.

I went home to prepare for my date with the most beautiful girl in the world. I reached for the best thing I had to wear—a two-piece, double-breasted silk suit I had. I put on my Armani cologne, and headed out to see my date. I entered the place, scanning the area, but could not see her. The bridal show began and everyone stood up, watching. From behind, I saw this blonde with these amazing legs, and knew it was her—she looked stunning. It so happened that I knew her friend, C.J., from my early teenage days. Everything was perfect.

Everyday thereafter, we saw each other. We went out to dinner, dancing, and the movies. Later, I met her family, and when they approved, she asked me to let my apartment go and move in with her. It was a tempting offer. She had a very nice place overlooking the Long Island Sound. Although I didn't have much, I was hesitant at first. I began thinking of the things I'd done, my patterns of behavior, and I didn't want this to just be a stepping stone. This was my first real apartment after being homeless that I could call my own, and if this didn't work, I would be ass out. It was an open invitation to a better life with a woman I was falling in love with. After much thought, I said okay, but I decided to rent the place out instead of giving it up, just in case.

I moved into her place. I was still working in the porn industry. Although she really didn't like it, she accepted it, and when I said I wanted to get out, she paid for some training to help get me into the counseling field. She would pack me some lunch and give me money for transportation. I began volunteering at Bronx Lebanon Hospital. I took more trainings, and went back to school to study becoming a substance abuse counselor. I got licensed and soon found a better job as a Research Specialist at Montefiore Hospital. I worked in the Palliative Care Program providing emotional support to patients, and families who were at the end of life stage with HIV/AIDS.

I opened up to Sky about my addiction and she didn't judge me. Instead, she supported me and even accompanied me to some NA meetings. At first it wasn't easy opening up. I was emotionally broken and didn't really trust anyone with my secrets. She soon helped me break down those walls with her kindness and understanding. I loved that she was so caring, so giving, and easy to get along with. I loved how she loved me. I became her everything and she became mine. She was funny, loving and man, did she talk a lot; most times she did all the talking—and really fast.

I began to see the world through her eyes; it was a much nicer place than the one I lived in. Her energy was amazing. She had no children, no baggage and no drama—I was a lucky man! My life came together because she helped me put the pieces in place. God sent me a good woman, as my mother always wanted for me, and I became a new man. I felt confident in telling her about my life and I began feeling that no matter what I shared, she loved and accepted me the way I was. My past interested her and she would always say how my life was like a movie. She helped me lose my fear and reaffirmed that my past was just a part of my story but not who I was entirely. With her, I began learning to live in the moment, slowly letting go of the past. Never did I think I would find, and become so deeply involved, with someone who would understand and support me in everything, who believed in me and who became my backbone no matter the outcome. As a result, my life forever changed.

We had so much in common. We took to traveling and exploring. It was because of her that I saw more than just NYC, Miami or Costa Rica. There was always something to do or somewhere to go.

No Regrets

I always said I'd never marry because I liked single life too much, but I wasn't going to let this one go. In my heart, I knew she was the right one. Life was going to be good. My family all adored her, and I'm sure my mother would've proudly approved and loved her. We made a great couple.

Returning from a trip to Puerto Rico, I arranged for all of her family and our friends to be at the house before we got there and wait quietly. It was a surprise. I got on one knee and I proposed to her. A year later, we were married. My cousin Mambo had just come home from prison in time for my wedding. I took him to buy some clothes, and put some money in his pocket—as we always do. At my wedding, he met my sister-in-law, they fell in love, and they never parted.

We were doing so well, I decided to start a jewelry business, and after that I started loan sharking. After work, I was running around collecting money, or having jewelry parties. It was work seven days a week, twelve to fourteen hours a day. Sky had a good job with the federal government and with both of our take home pay and all the money that was coming in from the businesses, we were on top of the world. We were living it up and making future plans. She was my partner and companion in life and she helped me get my life together. Throughout the years, she proved to have my back no matter the situation. What a great feeling having someone in my corner. Finally, all the goodness and righteous ways were paying off. God was showing me favor and blessing me every day.

My old flaws and habits began sneaking in on me. There was a time when again, I was battling with my identity and lustful behavior. I was beginning to feel suffocated and wasn't sure if I wanted to remain in this relationship, or life for that matter. My mind began to take over and agitate me, and I thought, "Maybe some time alone would be good." I needed to discover what was wrong and I couldn't do it there. I moved out into a friend's house to begin the single life all over again. After being in my longest relationship, I was a little apprehensive. The first few nights were difficult. After my wife did everything for me, I had to get used to taking care of myself again. I began to get the groove of it and looked forward to quiet nights, some soul searching and doing plenty of reading. I soon became lonely, and missed the comfort of a woman. Again my conscience became troubled. I distracted my mind through meditation and masturbation. After some time away, I decided I needed to be back home with my wife, the woman I could count on, the one who rode this out with me. I knew I hurt her and I wanted to make it up to her.

We talked and I went back home where I belonged. Although doubts entered my mind at times, I knew it was just me trying to run again and do what I had always done, convincing myself I wasn't happy enough. But now, just for today, I am standing still. Running is all I've ever done. I no longer have to live with those fears or insecurities. We've continued having our ups and downs, only now we work through them, and use counseling on some issues. Things may not always be great, but I am right where I need to be. Sky still continues to have my back as she always has. She has proven to be a real trooper with time. I am not easy when my mind keeps talking to me, but she gives me my space. Had it been another woman, I know I would've been gone for good. She truly loves me.

I'm still struggling with anger issues, and finding lasting peace, but I'm becoming more content with myself and my progress with life in general. I'm taking time to think, pause and not make the hasty decisions which always led to disaster. I can't expect miracles overnight, and I'll probably fall on my face a few more times before I get it right. Rome wasn't built in a day.

Getting it together.

CHAPTER 15

Freedom

was working for Montefiore Hospital making big bucks. It was the best job of my entire life. I loved it. My boss and the P-Care Team were the greatest group to work with. For the first time, I had no one telling me what to do and yet I took pride and did my work to the best of my ability. With my skills, I was able to move up quickly and I was told that I'd be given a new title with a higher salary, provided I went back to school because the new title required a master's degree. I enrolled in the College of New Rochelle. It became too difficult holding down all these jobs and going to school, so I chose to put it off till some time later, but that never happened.

During this period, I had a strong connection with a higher power and knew the doors were opening. My wife and I were doing well. We had enough money to invest in something for our future. We were both open to change. I loved New York, but I constantly feared getting busted for some mistaken identity, turning my whole world upside down. I saw it happening often and I didn't want to become another statistic.

This was the housing boom... The stock market was doing well. There was this big frenzy going on, a high energy period, and everyone was going crazy buying real estate and new homes. I took another trip to Florida to see for myself if I could get a feel for what was going on, and possibly find an investment opportunity.

It was just like I had heard. There was a certain excitement in the air. All kinds of homes were being built all over the place. People were scrambling to purchase homes. I too became excited by the energy, and fell into the same race looking for that perfect investment. I looked at many homes with these hungry realtors who were trying to get me to buy anything, and rushing me so they could move on to the next victim. All they saw was dollar signs. Most of them became very wealthy. I bought my very first home. I called my wife to give her the news that we were homeowners. It was a newly built, beautiful townhouse. My plan was to use it as an investment property, but I was going to enjoy it a little before I rented it. I went back home to work, and began making plans to return to Florida. When the house was finished, I took another trip.

It felt good. I was feeling a sense of pride. I was a kid from Brooklyn that never stopped dreaming, and here I was a homeowner. No one expected this. After being there a few days, my curiosity had me following some construction trucks which led me to some new model homes being shown to prospective buyers. I fell in love with one, and ended up putting a down payment on one of those too.

I was experiencing the most amazing feeling, second to being off drugs. I knew that once I got clean, I was destined for great things, but never thought purchasing my very own house was in the cards. I felt on top of the world—untouchable. The payoff was really happening, and fast at that. It was a natural high, and the world was the limit. Nothing could stop me now! "I was living the American dream." Look at me now, Mami…" I wished she was here to see how her little boy had grown into this wonderful man.

My excitement grew by the day. I was full of this newly found energy; I was feeling great, but I wanted more.

Immediately, I called my wife to share the joy. We were changing our lives, and moving out of N.Y.C. She put in a job transfer. I never thought I'd see the day. We were excited.

In 2005, I had resigned from my job, and we were moving forward with life's energy. I decided to take some time off to enjoy my home before I had to start figuring out what I wanted to do for employment. I had plenty of money, so I wasn't worried. Needless to say, my home became my new obsession. Although it was a newly constructed home, day after day, I looked for what else I could build or change to make it look better. It was like a new toy. I was able to sell our townhome for a good profit and, I was convinced by the realtor to roll it over into another property to avoid being taxed. I was so excited, I ended up buying three more investment properties.

One day, I was meeting with a realtor and banker from Country-Wide realtors, discussing how they could help qualify me when in reality my credit limit was already over the top. I remember thinking how special I was to get this preferred attention, but I didn't realize the shadiness of the whole deal. Soon after, the mortgage bubble burst and the housing market crashed. CountryWide went under for its bad practices, as did others. With the exception of our home, we lost all of our properties, and we filed for

Chapter 13 bankruptcy. So much money went down the drain. Now, I had to figure out how I was going to correct the situation and not sink. I kept my sanity, while many people were losing their minds, committing suicide, and suffering broken marriages due to investing their retirement accounts.

For me, it was just the way the cookie crumbled. If I had it twice, I could get it again. Only this time, it just didn't seem as important to me. I was beginning to sense, there was something much more important out there for me, but I didn't know what that was.

My criminal record was always in the back of my mind. It was easy for someone to look anyone up on Google and learn their whole history; this concerned me. It would be too much of a blow for someone to learn my secret, especially at this point in my life. I decided to try and see if I could get my record expunged.

Working through my previous parole officer and the State, I collected as many letters of recommendation as possible and, we submitted them to Governor Pataki of New York at the time. Prior to him leaving office, I was issued a certificate of relief restoring all my rights. An energy came upon me, and it was as though I got a new lease on life—a second chance to start over again.

With over twenty years of good behavior, I was able to go to school in Hoboken New Jersey, pass a test, and become a fugitive recovery agent, or bounty hunter. Upon graduation, I was given my own gold shield which looked just like a N.Y.C. detective—this blew my mind. These guys didn't know who I really was and they gave me a badge with an ID in a wallet. This could not be possible! I excused myself to go to the restroom just so I could look at it over and over again. It didn't seem real, I was dreaming I thought. I held it in my hand and I thanked God for making this possible.

It was the closest I was able to get to fulfilling my lifelong dream of being a police officer. My life had for sure turned around by leaps and bounds, and even I was surprised. It was a total 360 degree—I was living the dream. No one believed how I pulled this off.

I played the role and was excited doing so. I felt reborn. It felt so strange being on the other side now looking for bad guys. And because I had all the "bad guy," experience, I was good at it. It was all a power trip; my ego became inflated and I thought I was all that and a bag of chips. The convict in me was now buried forever, and there was no looking back.

I started working for the instructors at the school as a self-contractor, taking jobs in Florida looking for skip-fugitives, and bringing them back to the state they skipped from. Once, I took my prisoner, with his papers, to the county jail for holding until I was able to get him back across county lines. That was the weirdest feeling I ever experienced—going back into a jail—I was scared shitless. I was now looking at it from the other side.

No one knew me in Florida, so I was able to walk in many circles of law enforcement. They welcomed me into their groups as one of their own. We visited one another's homes, broke bread together, and had family barbeques and birthday parties. Just about all of my new friends were current cops or retired from New York. At first it felt a bit strange and I was a little preoccupied with it in my mind, wondering if they would ever find out who I really was, but they just seemed to accept me for who I was and soon my insecurities were dispelled. However, the fear always lingered in the back of my mind and I struggled with what I would say if anyone learned the truth. Although I was living a good life, and the mask had been somewhat put down; I realized then, I was still hiding behind it, and I worried about my past being revealed.

I continued to attend crime watch meetings at the police department every month and I even became a member of the Florida Association Crime Prevention, attending three-day weekend conventions they had throughout the state where all brass and high ranking members attended to strategize new prevention tactics—that really felt strange! Here I was, a known, former criminal among a sea of cops listening to privileged information. How ironic. Finally, I became an upstanding, respected member of society. I was respected not only in my community, but in the surrounding ones as well. I had put on community events and invited politicians, like the sheriff, state congressman, city mayor, city council and house of representative members to introduce them before elections—in which they all were successfully elected and are currently still serving. I also met with the deputy chief of police who lived in the community to help tackle certain issues. Everyone appreciated me. However, in the back of my mind, I always wondered— would they have ever dealt with me if they knew the secrets of my past. I was still wearing this mask.

No Regrets

I soon learned that the state of Florida didn't recognize "Bounty Hunters." Here they were called "Bondsman." I felt so discouraged when I learned I was in violation of the law, and that I had to go back to school to get licensed. So I did. I was getting all A's and B's. During my last class a guest speaker came to take fingerprints to submit to the state and I became paranoid. I pulled one of the teachers aside and confided in him that I had had previous encounters with the law. He told me that you cannot have ever been arrested or convicted of a felony to be a bondsman. I told him how I had heard it wouldn't be a problem because I was already in the field. He told me I could still submit my prints to see what would happen. My world came crashing down on me. I didn't want to open a can of worms and so I quit.

I became angry. I got in my car and took the lonely drive back home. I thought of still pursuing it, but decided to let it go. It was a difficult moment to process. I lived with it for a while; at least I knew I was still able to accomplish my dream. I did what many are not able to do. **Besides, I realized that covering a stake out in a van all night was sort of weighing on me and I wasn't sure how much longer I could take it.** I have to admit there were times when it was exciting as all hell. But, it was now time to move into the next chapter of my life.

CHAPTER 16

The Test

A couple of months later, while sitting and enjoying a nice evening with my garage door open, I noticed that the same guys that brought the appliances to the newly built houses were the same guys that I saw come and remove them later at two am in the morning. It was all suspicious to me and I knew something was going on so I kept an eye out. The activity continued and so I decided to take a visit to the local police department. I was told that the builder had to be the one to make the report. That same day I went to see the builder and told him what I saw. He confirmed that this had indeed been a problem that they had been aware of but they weren't sure who was doing it, and now they would try to correct it. From there on, the builder and I became friends, and he supported my efforts for my community. It was at that point that I became totally invested in my community and decided to serve selflessly. It became my way of giving back. I was a little uncomfortable having to go to the police and the builder. It was something I never thought I would have done, but I didn't want where I lived to become a lawless place, and someone had to stand up, so who better than me, since my past gave me insight into both sides.

I went to the police department and we started a crime watch program. Crime had been on the rise in Florida so the crime watch program had already been established throughout different communities and ours became an addition. Every month we held meetings at the police dept and I'd share that information with the community. I took charge, and recruited others to serve as block captains. I got deputy sheriffs, police officers and other neighbors who were invested in the community to serve. Everyone came together. We had meetings that grew by the week. On Halloween, we got on bikes with flashlights in our newly designed crime watch shirts to patrol the neighborhood and protect the children. I felt empowered, I felt pride and a great sense of purpose, because I was doing something meaningful. It was my way of giving back to society. The residents felt good to see what was going on and would come out in support. It was a great time in the history of our community. With the new text and email system we developed, we shared information and everyone was watching out. The community felt empowered. It was a great place to live.

We put on events in order for the neighbors to get to know one another and took turns walking the community making sure everyone was safe. Everyone was curious about this new movement being established. We got the speed bumps laid out which helped keep children safer while playing in the streets. We got stop signs, and more lighting throughout. We got an addition basketball court. We got a camera system at the front gate and pool area, and hired a security company. We monitored who came into the community as much as we could. I tried everything to help provide security for the families and community. We worked to modernize the front gates to minimize the codes from being given out to outsiders. We became a really active community, and set the standard for others to follow.

Years later, I helped set up committees and established the first ever home association in our neighborhood. We developed many projects to help uplift our community. It was a good place to live, until I began witnessing the drug dealing.

Coming from my background, the illegal activity was obvious. I could see things others couldn't, while most people had no clue what was going on. Late night when I couldn't sleep, I would take a stroll or ride my bike around the neighborhood, and sometimes I would see shady characters driving in throughout the night. During the day, I'd see some of these same cats. I would follow them to where they had gone to and get an idea of who these dealers were. There were more than three residents involved, and at times I would see those same residents congregating with one another—this was bigger than anyone knew. I lived directly behind the recreational area and could see everything that was going on. Once I noticed some illegal activity from a really good kid I knew who was getting caught up with a neighborhood thug. The kid's parents happened to be my next-door neighbors and were really nice people.

In order to try to save this kid, I decided to take him under my wing, and become his mentor. His name was Byron. I befriended him, learning his interests and aspirations. I knew he was an intelligent kid with good grades and not made for the streets. Since he lived next door to me, I'd see him all the time and we'd talk sometimes. One day I told him who I had seen him hanging with and I told him he should stay away from him. Soon enough,

the kid's parents called me giving me the news that their son had been arrested with another neighborhood kid for selling weed. They asked me for
my help. I knew a lot of people that looked up to and respected me. I made
a few phone calls, went to the courthouse, talked to the assistant district
attorney, and got the kid released. At this moment I knew this was going to
get out of control and I needed to put a stop to it. I went to see some of my
friends at the police department. They wanted to help me, but they were
understaffed, and because no real crime had occurred, they couldn't really
do anything. I went to the sheriff's department, and worked with my friend
in the community that worked with law enforcement, but they couldn't help
either because it wasn't in their jurisdiction. I contacted some of the politicians I knew, but they sent me back to the police.

I was beginning to feel hopeless. These drug dealers knew who I
was, where I lived, and that I was connected in some way with law enforcement. They tried to hide things from me and gave me respect. It felt strange
because I understood that life and I didn't want to snitch them out, and the
whole thing was making me feel uncomfortable.

I could feel this internal conflict with who I was before and who I
am now. I felt the new me being tested and I struggled with it. Even recruit-
ing block captains felt weird. I was still having inner conflict about the secrets of my past. I was once a part of the street culture and its code, and
snitching didn't feel normal. The streets did nothing but fuck my life up, and
now I was faced with doing the right thing and it was hard. However, my
neighborhood, and my family were more important than these thugs, who
only rented here and had no value for our property. I couldn't let this get out
of control in my own neighborhood.

One night, I approached some of them, and they denied it, but one
of their outsider friends got smart and challenged me. My anger rose and I
had to hold myself back from doing something I would have regretted. They
constantly drove into the community and would look at me hard all day long.
I knew how these kids think, and I also knew I was taking things too personal, and it began to get dangerous. Maybe it was my powerlessness which
was frustrating me and I couldn't let go of it. I was worried about one of
them firebombing my home one day, doing something to my family, or doing a drive by. Every day it was something or someone. I was becoming

obsessed, and annoyed as I kept witnessing the drug traffic on our street. I copied down hundreds of tag numbers in the event that something might happen and I'd have to go on a vigilante rampage. Something had to give. I was becoming tired of the blatant disrespect and knew I was taking a risk.

The peace I once felt was no longer. In a moment of prayer and meditation, I got my answer. To protect my family, I decided it was time to leave my home and everything that I had worked so hard for. It was either that, or go head to head with these guys until a crime was committed and the police department would come in and see it was a serious matter. It was not worth risking my life or freedom. I'd come too far now to lose everything I'd achieved. My personal growth and spiritual peace was priceless to me now. I was tempted to confront these kids and let them know who they were dealing with, but then, I realized I was no longer that reckless person whose buttons were so easy to push. I didn't need to prove something so badly that I'd end up in jail again. I wasn't giving my power away any longer. That alone was a huge accomplishment coming from the mentality I once had. My wife understood and we both agreed—it was time to let go. Even though the drug issues got worse, I remained committed to following through with our plan.

I had a garage sale to begin getting rid of our items. What we couldn't sell we gave away. I realized this stuff really didn't have value to me anymore anyway. We moved into a one-bedroom apartment with our two dogs. Leaving our home after all of the work, beautification, and money I put into it, was real difficult for us. We sacrificed and let go of everything, but it was probably one of the best decisions I've ever made to bring me happiness and peace. Chasing the illusion of having my own home with the white picket fence, had come to an end. Ultimately, I was freed from the stress of having a big home and all the work that came with it—it was more than I bargained for, and now time to let go, move on and free myself.

Maybe, it turned out to be a good thing, and it was all supposed to be this way. I came to understand it wasn't meant for me to tackle the issues with these drug dealers, but it gave me the opportunity to start the process to remove the mask that I had worn for so long. I followed God's direction. As I became more of myself, God began to put new things, new people and new ideas in me. I had a greater purpose to fulfill.

CHAPTER 17

The Battle Within

I didn't want to keep living in a battle with myself all the time. It was always difficult for me not to just do what I knew—reacting was my first instinct. Although it wasn't an easy process, when I realized the outcome that it's had on my life—the years of pain, suffering, and raw consequences; it became a no brainer. I lived a double life. My past choices were evidence that I had had no clear sense of direction, and I continued repeating the same mistakes. My losses were big, and my suffering unnecessary. Either I kept the path of pain and loss, or I made a change. I've come too far now to continue losing over senseless stuff. Too many of the good years had been lost—to give up more would be a waste of life.

I believe that I have gone through all of this for a reason. Although my experiences were painful blessings, I was meant to rise from the ashes and become the power of a better example. I have struggled with many issues not having a clue what to do, or if I would ever even get through, but I never gave up. Even when the pain was great and I was suffering, somewhere in my spirit I felt that one day it would all change and I would see the light of day again. I'm just the kind of person that always tried to find a solution and a way out. Many days I racked my brain, scared of sinking deeper into a place that I might not make it out of alive. I was forced to survive or die. After so many years stuck, my life seemed meaningless. I had no parents, uncles, aunts, friends or, brothers to help me—I was alone. No one gave me a hand out or a hand up. I had to con, manipulate, rob, sell drugs, and live hard core, using the skills the streets taught me to survive.

When the pain of that life became too much, and I decided to make a change, I switched it up and applied my survival skills to better my life, pushing to open doors, doing what I needed to do until I succeeded. I made sacrifice after sacrifice. I enrolled in every training or work preparation that was available through welfare, special assistance—whatever was free, I took the opportunity. Sometimes I didn't even eat so that I could get on a train to go to school or a training. Studying was not easy, nor was it what I wanted to do, but it was the work I had to put in for my new life that was long overdue. I was determined to succeed. If I survived the streets for as long as I had, nothing could stop me. The harder it got the more I pushed. There were many times I wanted to quit, but that was not an option—unless I was willing to go back to the life I had. Yes, I could blame my life and pain on my dad or others, but I couldn't go through life using that same excuse forever.

This was my life, and I needed to be the one to take control of it. This is what real troopers do. I was the surviving soldier. I've died many deaths, and crawled out of many holes. I was no longer a victim, nor was I looking for the meaning of life, as much as I was looking for the experience of feeling alive. I wanted to feel as one with life, and not against it. I wanted the energy of mother earth to flow through me so I could feel a part of it. I just wanted to let go of my fears and truly feel all that I could—good, bad or indifferent—and know I would survive. I wanted to make a difference if only to prove it to myself, to God, and to those that counted me out. I wanted to matter and go down like a soldier, not a chump. It was time to own up and become responsible for my actions.

This was an inside job and my own healing had to begin since dying was no longer an option. Death was not the greatest loss; the greatest loss was my spirit dying slowly inside of me while I lived. I found a new reason to want to live, and every day I woke up, I started off with that same drive. Suddenly, the smell in the air seemed different, the colors of the trees appeared brighter, the birds hummed in rhythm, and I was back in the flow of life. No longer were things a task, but a challenge, one that I was everyday looking forward to. The weights around my neck were gone, my spirit was lighter; I was reborn and full of energy, ready to take full advantage of my days.

One day, while at the beach walking my dogs, I had a moment to reflect. I looked back and said out loud, "Wow, after all I've done and been through, look where I've come to." Although it took me a while, I smiled and continued to enjoy a beautiful day. I am finally finding some peace.

My kids were now men, and there is not much I could do to change their ways, but my grandkids have hope. I want to build a relationship with them and correct some of the errors of my past. I want to teach them about life and hard work, watching they don't fall through the cracks of life, sucking them up like crumbs. I want to share my wisdom with them while they're young. I want them to be proud of their grandpa which survived the storm of his lifetime without falling to pieces. They need to feel loved, and understand that family is the greatest thing one can have. They need to know my story.

Maybe I can make a difference in someone's life that's fresh to the game, someone with whom I can share my life experience and knowledge. There is no excuse for bad judgment, or behavior. Wrong is wrong, and all humans understand this concept, and it is up to us to weigh out the consequences before the action. I have always paid a big price for my explosive, impulsive attitude. If only I could have been more aware of my emotions before I reacted. I allowed myself as a youngster to be easily swayed by others, and was caught up in admiring the cool cats in the hood, or so I thought. Not many scholars or scientists came from my hood. No one to look up to, but the suave, nicely dressed junkie, the thief that always seemed happy, the lover with all the girls, or the winos singing doo wop or acapella on the corner and in the subways stairs. These were the people I wanted to emulate. I can't remember being asked, "What would you want to be when you grow up." I learned to idolize the wrong things and wrong people. Life was more about survival, getting through the day, not dreaming or planning.

I could only hope to share my story with today's youth so they could learn from the choices I made and not have to suffer through the misery that awaits them if they follow that same path. It's too bad that most youth feel invincible and don't tend to listen too much—I understand this all too well.

The street life is like a world away from parents and all the shit at home. We'd go out to the streets and they'd become our teacher. It's so easy to get caught up in this when everyone in the hood is doing the same. I learned the hard way, and the people I should've trusted the most, became a mere shadow.

If I knew this were the price to pay, I probably would've trusted those who had my best interest—my family, as messed up as it was. Yeah, we were all dysfunctional, but it was all I had. I not only hurt myself, but my entire family. They suffered emotional pain, physical pain, and great financial loss. They paid for attorneys when in fact I was guilty, plus the cost of visiting me in upstate New York at the prisons and jails to bring me sneakers, or whatever little money they could for food and stamps. Everyone paid the price for my ignorance and stupidity. It ripped my family apart piece by piece, like the domino effect. Thereafter, I came home to separation, family illness and death. I watched as my family legacy came crumbling down and I felt helpless. Everyone in my family is almost gone now. Those that remain are either physically ill, or mentally jacked up, or live far away and it's like they're not even there.

All along, there was a pattern which I failed to acknowledge that trickled down drip by drip and destroyed everything in its path. There is no reset button or do-overs. I often wonder if there was something I could've done earlier to change the outcome. I wonder where I would be if God had not rescued me... I had to be brought to my knees before I made the change.

Now I see time as precious, what little of it there is. Where have all the years gone? Everything and everyone look so different. I look in the mirror at my aging face and body, and although I can still see that little boy and feel his pain, everything seems so far away. Now I try in my old age to play catch-up, but what's gone, is gone forever; as difficult as it is. Did it have to be this way? I look at my baby picture—the only one I have, and I tell the little boy, "I am here as the adult for you today, to take care of and love you, that you are enough, and I will take care of us from here on out— you will no longer have to suffer." It is time for the boy to come out, laugh and play, the teenager to be happy and content, and the adult to be in peace and find his joy.

If only I could live a hundred years more and make right all the wrongs. If there was only one thing left for me to do, it would be to love those that love me, to bring healing to what's left of my family, and to those in the world around me. We all have been hurt by life's circumstances in some way or another. Many of us carry grudges and pain in our body. We don't forgive easily, or let go, and if we stay in battle with ourselves, we can become very sick psychologically and emotionally. The self-hate becomes a toxic poison that we're immune and conditioned to; this is easy for us because it's all we ever knew to do, and most times we are not even aware of it, as if it was the norm. As the clock keeps ticking, life evades us and we grow old.

I want to cherish the few moments I have left on earth, and to one day find my peace. I still have no regrets, although; there are some things I wish I've would've done differently. The error of those mishaps will follow me forever, and it is the cross I must carry until my very last breath.

Everything in life has its own timing, and for whatever reason—it is the way it's supposed to be. Today I live in the moment, I have accepted all that is the way it is. "It is what it is" Neither I nor anyone else can change the past; we can only try to be the best person we can and learn from our mistakes. If I allow myself to truly feel my feelings, I can let go and they too will come to pass. I just have to hold on and walk through the pain without resistance. Most times, it is at that deep level where my greatest lessons have been learned. The message is not always clear, sometimes even hidden, but it is there. A wise man not only learns from his mistakes. Our choices determine our path. We all have the power of choice, so it is important to choose wisely.

My wife and I have prepared ourselves for telling my story and how it could potentially impact our lives. I have taken many risks by revealing myself. I may even be ostracized by an entire community, including many of our friends. Dying with the secrets of my past, hidden behind my mask, would have truly buried my soul, and I knew my responsibility was to heal so that I can leave this earth with a healthier spirit than what I inherited.

My award.

CHAPTER 18

My Reward

Thirteen years later, I was called back to the community by my friend who was the new HOA president and the board members. They honored me with a plaque with my name etched on a stone monument pillar at the newly built children's playground. It was all in recognition of my thirteen years of selfless volunteer service. That was one of the greatest rewards of my life. The first reward was when Byron, the kid in Florida I used to mentor, came to tell me he was in college and heading to China to work as an English Teacher.

After many years passed, I got a call from California—it was Harry. I was able to take a trip to San Francisco and spend two weeks with him and his brother Herb. It was a long-awaited reunion and our friendship rekindled. So much catching up in so little time. It felt a little strange at first sharing our successes and not the war stories we both had once identified with. We had walked many paths together and alone. We are different men now, neither one of us should still be here after all the battles and sacrifices we've gone through. He has become successful as a youth counselor in California working with youth in gangs helping to save lives—how ironic is that! God has a sense of humor. Forty-eight years later, we are still as important to one another as the day in that alley where we first made that pact.

Two years ago in 2016, Harry invited me to attend a red carpet event in New York City for the premiere of the movie "Wall Writers," which chronicled the graffiti era and included his early work as a pioneer of that movement. We couldn't believe the line of people waiting to get Harry's signature. Graffiti artists came from all over the world to see the film and meet him. I was so proud of him and our neighborhood homies. I had been writing a little here and there about my life in a notebook, but it was that night that Harry inspired me to fully write my story. Today, he continues to motivate me while encouraging me to never quit.

Life for sure has come full circle. I may not have the best explanation for why things happened the way they did or my reaction to the circumstances. It was the hand I was dealt and I played it the only way I knew how.

The experiences shaped who I was, and I can't say I regret any of it, because then I probably wouldn't be who I am today.

I am no longer ostracized from life, but I am one with life. I am getting closer to the man I want to be. I have lived a lifetime in search of something, just to find out all along it was inside of me and that nothing else really matters. Life is not always good or fair, but it is a gift. Follow your spirit, and live out your dreams. Nothing is ever too late!

Now, the secret is out, the mask is off and I have the courage to say "Judge me as I am, not for whom I was"… I am FREE! I have NO RE-GRETS!

Me and Henry in the old hood.

EPILOGUE

ocked in a fantasy world full of illusion and lies, believing in what I saw or heard, the streets became my teacher. I believed in a lie for so long that I was afraid to look at the truth. My only goal became boosting my image and power. I was obsessed and consumed with wanting more and didn't care about the consequences. I was in denial, thinking it would be different if I did it another way. Controlled by my ego, I was constantly in an internal struggle with myself. All along, my conscience was knocking, but I refused to listen. Spiritually I was dead. There was no life left in me. I became miserable in my own skin. I went in circles and could not find a way out from the lost world I was trapped in, and I kept repeating the same things over and over again, day after day, month after month, and year after year, I watched time turn into decades and I remained stuck.

So much time wasted, caught in the abyss of a disease that was stronger than anything I imagined. It ruled me and took me into the dark corners of hell. I walked among people that when you looked into their eyes, you could see nothing but a blank stare like zombies. The person I saw in the mirror was a total stranger. I continued walking among the ghosts in search of nothing and chasing the wind. I was totally defeated and at the end of my rope.

Addicted to the lifestyle that came with the game, and confined to a prison I'd created in my own mind, I became the hostage of my own making. Street life became the way- it embraced and controlled me. I carried the burden of the little child within me, dictating my life because he was hurt, while the angry teenager kept rebelling, and the confused adult was miserable. He used everything and everyone he could to stop the noise in his head and numb the pain through sex, money and drugs. The secrets held me hostage daily, and blocking the pain was my only mission. I created my own hell on earth.

From a power deep within, I finally made the decision to free myself from my self-destruction and take action. I chose the road to change. That was my first breakthrough. The walls to climb were tall, but I was determined, and I couldn't keep hurting myself. In the darkest of times, I was faced with myself, no longer able to run, I decided it was now or never. I needed to find that place where I would be safe. As I hit my knees and in total desperation, I turned to God, and I felt a flicker of hope. I begged God to give me one more chance to start anew - he heard me. I knew I could do this. I would probably fall on my face a few times because of doubt or insecurity, but I chose to continue despite all I would encounter. I finally was willing to pay whatever price I needed to. From that point on, things became better. I changed my thinking and convinced myself I could do this.

Even today, forty-five years later, I still see the faces of the people I've hurt during my street battles, and the nightmares of being back in prison still haunt me. Many nights I dream I'm fighting, hearing gunshots, being stabbed and chased, or hearing the horrors of the sexual abuse and cries of others, and I wake up in a cold sweat. The streets were hard core and they carried a price. Many of my victims had families as well, and they were also affected by the choices I made. I had to come to terms with those decisions, and work hard to forgive myself. I've never stopped praying for those families whose lives I've wrecked. It's barbaric how everyone suffers in the game, but we keep playing. It's never easy, and the healing process is slow coming. After years of recurring nightmares, I finally sought help and was actually diagnosed with post-traumatic stress disorder, or PTSD. I am not sure of God's plan for me, but I try to keep still enough to listen. Today, I accept responsibility, remain positive, and look for reasons to feel alive. It is because of God's grace that I am here to share my story with you, when I should've been dead long ago. Today that flicker of hope still shines brightly, as I renew my commitment every day to keep the light on.

There is very little that I complain about today. I am blessed beyond my wildest dreams. In writing my story, I had to do a lot of soul-searching. I questioned whether I wanted to relive my past by experiencing some of the traumatic and painful moments over again. The more I dug, the stronger the feelings were, and tears rolled down my face. Everything is still as fresh as yesterday. It never gets easier; I just learn to bury the thoughts and move on. No matter how much I tried to escape by running, the mask always followed, and eventually the past would catch up. Much effort has been put into the shattering of the mask, and although some fragments remain, for the most part, it has been put to rest, and I've been able to restore some sanity. Difficult as it is, the work continues, and I must free myself from the many masks I've worn so that I can finally embrace and live as my true self.

It wasn't easy having to make the choices I did with no one there to guide or mentor me. Everything I had suffered and the decisions I made were a direct result from that one childhood experience which afflicted me throughout my entire life. It was those feelings that I carried with me for 45 years, the ones I constantly tried to run from, separating me from humanity, causing me to create the many masks I'd worn. No jail could have detained my soul as bad as the prison I had locked myself into. Those were the tallest walls I had to climb over and nothing could have been more challenging. It is truly a miracle for anyone to have survived an emotional and spiritual storm for that long.

I've come to terms with the fact that I hurt many people and used many women. I realize that I was never a gangster, but I pretended to be one out of fear and mere survival. Manipulation, deceit, and acting like a con-man became second nature. It was always about what I wanted and no one could stand in my way. I was disgusted with myself and I trusted no one. My story is not about the crimes, but about my struggles, my secrets, my tunnel vision, and the irrational thinking that came from a hurt closed-minded child, whose defects carried into adulthood. But, my story is also about my success and the great lessons that came from the breakthrough and the challenge in my quest for love and peace. The painful experiences obstructed my vision and so I didn't really know what love or peace was. It is no wonder that kids with no positive influences or role models find themselves lost. From the onset, everything is an uphill battle that becomes very complex for a child who can easily be steered in the wrong direction. I was an angry, lost and rebellious little boy with no direction, in search of his mother's love in every woman he encountered, wanting to be held and given a chance. The healing process has to go back to when the pain first began—with that little child. It may well be the healing of that child that has become my life-long journey.

I am far from being enslaved in a 6 x 9 jail cell where I spent a big portion of my life. It's about finding me and the inner journey. I pray to never forget the lessons. It is through those experiences that I've obtained what little wisdom I have. I am no longer bitter or angry, but instead tranquil and content. God has provided all of my needs and then some. I have been given a third chance to redirect my life and leave the world a better place. Everything in life has a purpose; pain, suffering, death, and even love. This is no longer about anyone else, but about me. I understand now I had to die a thousand deaths, so that I can live just this one.

It's about the feelings, and allowing myself to walk through the pain without resistance. For they, like all else, will come to pass. I just have to hold on and ride out the storm. Whether it is a broken heart, growing pains, or raw experiences, I know "this too shall pass," and I will get through whatever it is. The lessons for me were hard, and they'll continue to come, but I no longer run. No one promised me a pain-free life; pain has a way of clipping one's wings when they were meant to fly free. I am that eagle with tattered wings that never flew, but now soars. Nobody would say, "look that eagle has ugly wings." No they would say, "look at that eagle, it's a miracle that it's still alive and rising." The potential to be free has always been within me, and although I don't have the power to change the past, I accept it for the way it is. Life does not happen without struggle, but I'll keep smiling. I will continue trying to find a place within where there is joy, so that the joy can burn the pain. My life and experiences were not in vain. Now, I know there was a greater purpose.

It is that purpose I now seek. I can and will overcome whatever life throws at me. For me, death is not the greatest loss - the greatest loss is what dies inside me while I live. I can truly now say, "I've come into manhood!"

In retrospect, looking back at my family history, my father loved me as he did us all. Despite all the bad he did, he was a good man and a protective father. His father probably treated him the same and his grandfather, his father. I can see now he was caught up in a family cycle of abuse. There were days he was better, and I choose to remember those times. Being an alcoholic only brought the worst out of him. With most of my siblings caught in some form of addiction, I knew that I too would likely be bound to follow that path of suffering unless something drastic occurred to disrupt the pattern. I've made some bad choices and paid a heavy price. Everything I thought I knew has been subjected to revision.

There is plenty of work to do in order to grow and move into the next phase of my journey. I'm still discovering my purpose in life. What I am sure of is that I needed to see how my defect of character has ruled my life, and it had to take some nuclear blasts to rebuild it over again. I have learned many lessons. I can now better understand myself, my reactions, and my emotions. No matter how difficult those lessons were, they became the gateway to my healing. The best thing I could've done was to open my arms to it and embrace whatever it was. It was that acceptance and surrender which got me through. This is how I live my life today, and although never easy, it is better. I offer no resistance to what is, and take one day at a time and that's the best I can hope for.

Today the most valuable thing I have is my spirit, and when I'm not right within, I'm miserable. I am learning to allow the present moment to be and to accept the impermanent nature of all things and conditions. When I live in complete acceptance of what is, there is peace, and this calms any drama that may arise in my life. My concept of love and affection has always been twisted, and all the things I thought I knew I had to unlearn. I had to rewire my brain with new information, incorporate better choices and responsible behavior. I am no longer ostracized from life, but one with life. I have found a sense of belonging and am happier with being me. Today I am definitely in a better place. Peace has been elusive, but I've seen enough glimpses of it to continue seeking it out. Finding purpose and peace is my lifelong journey.

In my worst pain, came the greatest growth and I am grateful for the painful blessing. Today I live a humble life in my own home with my loving wife and two dogs. Despite all the struggles, we have been fortunate and blessed. If my God were to call me today, I would go without resistance. I am no longer afraid; I live in the moment. I will continue to be the best person I can, and share as much love as I can until I am called home.

Every day I ask my God for forgiveness for the pain I have caused others, for my judgement of others, and for my shortcomings. My amends will go on forever; to my father who did the best he could, and gave me what he had through what he knew. To my mother who I gave a hard time and died a lonely death never being able to see her son living well and prospering. I miss you Mami so much and I love you. It is your picture on my desk, when I look at your eyes staring at me, that tells me, you love me too, and that you are with me always. To my children, particularly my two boys who never understood me because of my lack of communication skills, tolerance, stubbornness and lack of patience. It was always my way and my point of view. To the police officer I hurt and his family. To my friends that may be hurt through my honesty and self-disclosure. To all the good women in my life that loved me, and those I've hurt because of my selfishness, or self-centered ways. To my loving wife for sometimes falling short as the best husband I could be while she stood by me.

I wrote this so I could tell this story through my eyes, my truth. I wanted my boys to learn about my struggle and I told it as honestly as I could. This is not a full and complete story, and some things were left out so as not to directly hurt anyone. I am sure some will never forgive me, and that's fine as well. I hope we all find the power to move on. I wish you all the freedom from what keeps you stuck.

As I continue my journey of self-exploration, I hope whatever I do and have done can make a difference in someone's life.

The errors of my life may not be over. So much has been lost and gone forever. I can't change what happened, but I can stop the bleeding by not repeating my mistakes. Let's forgive, so we can live.

"After the tears comes the joy."

Me working as a bounty hunter.

I CANNOT RUN FROM ME

ABOUT THE AUTHOR

It was very difficult to write this book and I had a lot of apprehension. I was afraid it might surprise and hurt people, but this is truly who I am. I felt the need to free myself from the secrets and the demons which held me hostage all my life. I lived a lie and the burden of the mask I wore kept me sick. It helped me cope with my insecurities, and the need to be socially accepted. I ran from life by putting myself in this impenetrable bubble out of the realms of society. I created unnecessary pain not understanding it was me I was hurting. I was living a lie and needed to be free.

I am hoping to reach others that have suffered, or still are suffering with shame and guilt. I hope to bring a message of hope and acceptance to those that are still struggling.

I've been able to accomplish many things I could have only dreamt about:

I became a Licensed International Addiction Counselor helping others as it has been my passion in life.

I invented a Medical Orthopedic Device and was awarded a US Government Patent.

I've started various businesses.

The Governor of The State of N.Y. awarded me a Certificate of Release. As a result I was able to become a Fugitive Recovery Agent.

I am a certified locksmith.

I served for nine years as a coordinator for the Crime Watch Program in our community, and I am a former member of the Florida Crime Prevention Association.

And most of all, I am the real Pepe Santos without the mask.

No regrets.

LIST OF CHARACTERS

1. Pepe Santos - me
2. Pop - Dad
3. Mom- Mom
4. Cindy - little sister
5. Mimi- first girlfriend
6. Curtis, Ray, Teddy, Sally Paulie, Clyde - grammar school friends
7. Jimbo - big brother
8. Mary - ex sister-in-law
9. Nelly - Mary's sister
10. Ray, Larry - friends in Brooklyn
11. Victor - uncle
12. Harry - best friend
13. White Mike - tagging/ train accident
14. Terry - childhood sweetheart
15. Andrea - first son's mother
16. Anthony - first son
17. Renzo - ex brother-in-law
18. Alex - second son
19. Ed - brother
20. Dee - sister
21. Will - president Latin Demons
22. Nick - VP Latin Demons
23. Danny - gang member artist
24. Mambo - cousin
25. Joey - best friend
26. Mick - Joey's brother
27. Lollipop - gay friend
28. Bella - 2nd sons Mom

29. Freddy - jailhouse friend
30. Mario - Italian on Baseball team
31. Girlfriend - no name
32. Jimmy - drug connection to Dominicans
33. Sister's friend - no name
34. Joe - Colombian connection in sister's case
35. Marleen - Mambo's girl, nurse from Harlem Hospital
36. Sal - ex brother-in-law
37. Yolanda - girlfriend
38. Byron - Neighborhood kid
39. Sky - wife